## Praise for *The Box of Da*

"I thoroughly enjoyed every page of *The Box of Daughter*. This book changes you. You'll walk away more compassionate and inspired to live your best life."
—**Ellen Padnos, Women.com**

"An excellent book to give to a friend struggling with family entanglement issues.... I have no doubt it will help many, many people."
—**TCM Reviews**

"A hopeful story of a woman unraveled by abuse but found again in self-love and recovery."
—**Karyl McBride, Ph.D., author of *Will I Ever Be Good Enough? Healing the Daughters of Narcissistic Mothers***

"Mayfield's memoir is a testament to the merit of psychological healing through the understanding and expression of feelings. Full of stark realities of abuse but also the hopefulness of healing, Mayfield's memoir provides helpful insight to those facing similar struggles."
—**Kirkus Reviews**

"Fresh, bold, and inspiring."
—**Examiner.com**

"This book stirred up a lot of "aha" moments—oh look, that's my mom...oh look, that's my whole family! Well-written, intriguing, and so very enlightening. Thoroughly enjoyed this book, and if I could give it more than 5 stars, I certainly would."
—**LibraryThing**

"A very compelling and honest account of the author's growing self-awareness and ascent from a lifetime of abuse."
—**Toadstool Bookshop, Milford, NH**

*"The Box of Daughter* is a fine pick for community library memoir collections focusing on the family."
—**Midwest Book Review**

**Also by Katherine Mayfield**

*The Box of Daughter and Other Poems*
*Smart Actors, Foolish Choices*
*Acting A to Z*
*The Last Visit*

"Katherine Mayfield's book is an insightful, honest, and riveting account of her childhood emotional abuse and her journey to wholeness as an adult."
**—Aletha Solter, Ph.D., founder of the Aware Parenting Institute and author of *Tears and Tantrums***

"Katherine Mayfield holds nothing back, and her unflinching, thorough, and articulate honesty is a true gift for anyone wanting to understand, face, and rise above the emotional scars of a damaging childhood."
**—Amy Wood, Psy.D., author of *Life Your Way***

"A brave, unflinching, and exquisitely rendered memoir of a family caught in the tragic and relentless cycles of emotional incest. Couldn't put it down."
**—Darcy Scott, author of *Hunter Huntress* and *Matinicus***

"Katherine Mayfield has tackled the elusiveness of corrosive parenting by pulling back the layers with her fine writing. We are all the better for it."
**—Jacqueline Sheehan, New York Times bestselling author of *Lost & Found* and *Now & Then***

# The Box of Daughter

## Healing the Authentic Self

*Katherine Mayfield*

A memoir by
Katherine Mayfield

Second Edition.

ISBN 978-1-936447-43-5

Permission to use quote from *Tears and Tantrums* granted by Dr. Aletha Solter of the Aware Parenting Institute, Galena, CA.

Permission to use quote from *Steering by Starlight* granted by Martha Beck, www.marthabeck.com.

**Author's Note:**
This is a book about the workings of the psyche as much as it is about my relationship with my parents. Each individual psyche has its own unique process of recording events and experiences, and I have written this story as best I can from the memories stored within my neural network and physical self. Some names and locations have been changed to protect individual privacy.

The process of healing outlined in *The Box of Daughter* is based on the work and writings of Alice Miller, particularly her books *The Drama of the Gifted Child, For Your Own Good,* and *The Body Never Lies.*

Maine Authors Publishing
Rockland, ME

*To Tamar S. and Kathi D.:*

*Without your help, my deepest self*
*would still be locked inside the box.*

*And to all those who have been emotionally abused:*
*It wasn't your fault, and you are good enough.*

# Contents

# The Box of Daughter

When I was a little girl,
I wanted more than anything
To be a person.
But my parents wanted me
To be a daughter.
"We put you in the box of daughter," they told me,
Though not in so many words,
And having no choice,
Because I *was* a daughter,
I climbed into the box.
I didn't like it there, but it felt safe.

The box of daughter was small and dark,
There wasn't much air,
Or personhood,
And not very much life could get
Into or out of the box.
There wasn't enough room
For all the parts of me,
So I had to leave some of myself
Outside the box.
Then I forgot where it was.
(Or someone threw it away when I wasn't looking.)

My brother was the lucky one—
He was in the box of son.
He got to do what he wanted
(Though sometimes he got punished for it,
But I guess that was the price of
Being in the box of son and doing what you wanted).
I don't know if he's still in the box now;
He lives in L.A.

It's been many years now
That I've been in the box of daughter—
I've worked a lot on the box,
Making holes to see out,
And so that more light and life can come in.

I've pushed and pushed at the walls for years and years,
Trying to make the box fit me better,
But it's a very strong box.

I've tried just stepping out of the box sometimes,
And sometimes it works,
But I'm afraid it will cause my parents pain
And they already seem to have
Too much to cope with.
How can I hurt people
Who are already hurting too much?
That would make me feel cruel.
And so I live on in the small, dark box of daughter.

I hope one day long before the end of my life
I'll be set free from the box.
I'm so excited to find out one day
What life is like
Outside the box of daughter.

K.M.  1999

—from *The Box of Daughter and Other Poems*

# Chapter 1:  Looking Out for Number One

The September wind is chilly and damp. It slices through my jacket, raising goosebumps on my stick-thin body as I stare at the tombstones marching silently in rows between the trees and down the hill, like frozen soldiers with no battle left to wage. My father's ashes are freshly buried beside my mother's. The time has come for the final goodbye.

I don't have words for all I need to say. My parents used up so much of me throughout my life that I don't know who I am. The part of me that thought I had to die so that my parents could live stands bewildered that I made it through. After seven years of caregiving, there's nothing left of me. I feel as if I've fought a battle for my life.

I push my feelings aside for a moment to say a prayer for my parents, that God may grant them peace in return for their lifelong gifts of service to others. Indescribable relief washes over me as I realize that after fifty years of living in the box of daughter and struggling to escape the abuse, I'm free at last to find myself and live my life.

I've been unraveling the tapestry of my childhood for two decades now:  combing through the warp and weft, the tightly knotted patterns of my family's dysfunction; examining the colors of the tattered threads and the roots of the design to finally stumble on and understand the place from which I've come. For twenty years, I've struggled with every fiber of my being to find out who I am beneath the tangle of ideas and beliefs and rules and regulations I was taught.

And as I turn away from my parents' graves and take my first step toward freedom, I realize that my journey has only just begun.

\* \* \*

The first thing my mother taught me was that whining was the worst thing in the world, a crime nearly equal to making reference to private parts. She started my training early, when I was three or four years old.

*In my memory*, it's a warm summer day. The air smells green, and makes my nose tingle. We've gone to the post office, the library, and the church, and now we're shopping in the grocery store. I like the grocery store, with all the colored packages and people pushing their carts up and down the aisles, making choices that are different from my mother's. But I'm getting tired. My back hurts from sitting in the cart, and I want to lie down.

"Can we go home now, Mommy?" I long for bear and bed.

She's holding two cereal boxes in her hands, looking back and forth from one to the other. She looks nice today in her sleeveless green polyester top and brightly flowered skirt. "I'll be done shortly, then we'll go home."

I raise the volume a little, hoping to get her attention and make her understand the enormity of my need.

"But I'm sleepy, Mommy. I want to lie down."

Her eyes start shifting this way and that, looking to see who might be noticing who has a whiny child. Her broad shoulders hunch and her neck starts to disappear. She carefully places the boxes back on the shelf, and I notice people looking at us. Their faces frown, their bodies seem to threaten. The bad feelings coming from my mother poke at me like hot needles as she stands way up above me, her dark curly hair looking almost black against the bright grocery store lights. She leans down too close to me, not looking at me, but looking out at the public, where the importance is. She grabs my hand with her big, knobby one, and squeezes it until it hurts. My breath stops in my chest.

"Your whine is showing," she says quietly in her threatening sing-song voice, as if it's the most incredibly shameful thing in the world to have one's whine showing. I never want to shame myself like that again, and I want her to stop squeezing my hand, so I start turning into the Good Little Girl.

"I'm sorry, Mommy," I plead. "I won't whine anymore." I try to pull my hand back, but my mother won't let go.

"That's a good little girl," she says. "Remember, God is watching you." She gives my hand a little yank before letting it go, and then she stands up and pushes her glasses back up on her nose before going back to the cereal boxes.

I take in a breath as I put my sore hand between my legs.

Now I know that what I want is bad, and all that's important is what other people think.

I will absolutely remember never to complain again.

I loved to read stories when I was small. I loved the thrill of imagining other places and wondering how other people lived their lives. Jack and the Beanstalk, Snow-White and Rose-Red, Cinderella—stories gave me a look into worlds that were different from the world I lived in. When my mother or father read to me, I took on the roles of the characters, playing Jack as he shinnied up the beanstalk, or poor Cinderella slaving under the cruel and watchful eye of her stepmother. It was so much more exciting to be someone else than to be myself.

My parents nicknamed me "Princess," and deep down underneath all of my fear and uncertainty, I thought I should be one. I imagined standing on a balcony in front of cheering crowds, seeing smiles on the faces of people who loved me. I imagined being respected and appreciated, sharing warmth and affection with other people the way characters did in some of the stories I read. But over the years, the nickname "Princess" simply became another label for the Good Little Girl, trotted out whenever my parents wanted to turn me back in their direction:

"Princess, would you come here and help me set the table?"

"Now, Princess, don't complain."

"Be a Princess and fetch my slippers for me, will you?"

"Don't argue, Princess, just do what I say."

I knew happiness was possible, because sometimes I saw other people who looked like they were enjoying themselves. So I waited, day after day, for the turning point in the story when everything would start to get better and home would become a happy place.

When I was five, my mother taught me how to plant flowers.

It's a bright fall morning, the sunlight drenched with the reflection of glorious red and yellow leaves. The crisp, cool weather lifts my mother's customary pessimistic mood.

"Let's go plant some flowers," she says.

We go out to the garage and get some tools for digging holes and a paper bag of flower bulbs she got from the hardware store this week.

"You'll like planting flowers," she says, her voice lilting. "It's a lot of fun."

I love seeing the flowers when they come up— the nodding yellow daffodils, the purple hyacinths with the smell I love, the pink roses on the small rosebushes curling their petals into beautiful swirls of color and light and shadow. I imagine it will be fun to plant them, as if I'm gently putting them to sleep so they can grow strong and make even more beautiful colors.

I follow my mother out the back door of the garage to a spot next to the white picket fence that separates the neighbor's yard from ours. My mother drops the bag and tools on the ground, places an old towel down next to them, and kneels on the towel.

"Here. This would be a good place for the flowers. Why don't you dig the first hole?"

I kneel down on the ground next to her, and pick up the trowel. I like the feel of it in my hand, like I could conduct a symphony with it.

"No, no, that's not right. Hold it this way." She takes the trowel, and turns my hand up, placing the trowel in it. I twist my arm and shoulder so I can point the trowel at the ground, shove it into the soil, and pull up the dirt. The warm, moist smell of the earth drifts up, offering the same kind of comfort as my bear when I bury my nose in his fluffy, brown fur.

"No, not there. Make the hole over here." I put the dirt back in the hole, and move the trowel over a few inches to where my mother is pointing.

"Here?" I look up at her, wanting to make sure I've got the right spot.

"Yes. Go ahead." I push the trowel in again, and pull out the dirt. I start to drop it next to the hole.

"No, don't put the dirt there, we're going to dig there next." Her voice sounds tight, like she can't get it out. "Put it over here." She taps on the ground, and I carefully move the trowel with the dirt in it and dump it next to where she's tapping.

"Bigger. Make the hole bigger. It has to be deeper." I keep digging, putting the dirt all in the same pile.

"Round out the edges." I don't know what she means.

"What?"

She lets out a small hiss of annoyance, and her voice rises. "Round out the edges. Make it round."

"Like a ball?"

"No, no, no, no! Here, let me do it." She reaches for the trowel.

I pull away. "Mommy, I want to finish the hole so I can put the flower in it."

She grabs my arm and yanks me back behind her. As she jerks the trowel away from me, she says, "You're not doing it right!" Then she says, "Ouch!" and rubs one of her bulging knuckles, because it hurts. Her arthritis is bad today. She purses her lips and frowns at me through the pain. I didn't mean to hurt her. I watch as her broad shoulders and strong arms work to smooth the edges of the hole so it looks like a circle. Now I understand about making it round.

A cloud of badness rises inside me. "I'm sorry, Mommy. I'll do better next time." My hand aches to take the trowel again, to carry the rich, brown earth from one place to another, to put a bulb to sleep the way I tuck my dolls in at night.

She doesn't look at me. Her anger jumps at me like jagged bolts of lightning, and my nerves start to tingle. "I'm sorry, too," she snaps. "Now you go play in the sandbox. I'm going to finish planting the flowers."

I try not to whine. "But I want to plant one."

"No, you can't do it. Now go play." She takes a bulb from the sack, and gently places it in the hole before scooping the dirt back on top of it and patting it tenderly. I wish she would touch me like that. I want to watch her plant the rest of the flowers, but I turn away and go to the sandbox.

I make some little hills of sand with my hands. I'm not good enough or smart enough to even plant flowers, and I don't know how to do better. I can feel my mother's arms and hands as she digs the holes, puts the bulbs in, covers them with dirt, and gently pats them to sleep. I look over at my mother across the yard, her back to me, planting the flowers I wanted to plant. I get up and go over to her, wanting to fix it somehow.

"Mommy?"

She ignores me as she pushes her dark wing-tipped glasses back up on her nose with her forearm and keeps digging. I pull up my courage and try to think of an important question.

"Mommy, how long does it take for the flowers to come up?"

She sighs and drops her arms to her sides, and her voice is quiet and sad as she looks at the ground. "They'll come up in the spring. Now go play." I can tell that she wants something, really badly, but I don't know what it is.

I want to know how long until spring comes, and what makes the flowers come out of the bulbs, but I go back to the sandbox, and make more little hills. When my daddy is here, he brings a pail of water so I can make the sand wet. Then I can build castles with doors and windows.

I look over at my mother again, and I realize that if I don't do exactly what she wants, she'll send me away and I'll be all alone. I vow that from now on, I will ignore what I want, and do my best to give her whatever she wants.

Suddenly, my mother is standing next to the sandbox, making a tall shadow over the sand hills. I look up at her.

"What are you making?" she asks. Her hair looks like a dark cloud against the blue sky. Her dark eyes stab into me like a long needle, and I get goosebumps.

"A castle," I say. "But I need some water."

"It's not very big."

"It doesn't stand up without water. Could you get me some?"

"Did you want to plant the last flower?" she asks.

I look down at the sand, trying to figure this out. She said I couldn't plant flowers. Is this a trick? Sometimes she likes to trick me.

I can feel her looking down at me. Usually I know what she's thinking, but I can't tell this time. I look up at her and nod slowly, not sure whether I'm making the right answer.

"Come on, then." She turns and walks back toward the fence. I follow her, wondering why I couldn't plant a flower before, but now I can, and why she didn't want me, but now she does. Maybe it's because I was good, and went to play when she told me to.

I kneel down at the last hole my mother has made. I remember how my mother planted the flower bulb, and I hope I can do it right. I want her to be proud of me, to smile a nice smile at me, to make us both happy. I reach in the bag for the last bulb, place it gently in the hole, and pick up the trowel.

"No, turn the bulb over so the point is up."

I did it wrong. But if I know why, I can remember to do it right next time. "Why?" I ask.

"Just turn it over." Her voice rises. I made her mad again. I reach into the hole with my other hand, turn the bulb over, and look up at my mother. She nods. I scoop the dirt from the pile into the hole, scooping and scooping until it's full. Then I pat the top with the trowel, the way she did.

"Okay." She hands me the paper bag and gets up. "Throw this in the garbage." I take the bag over to the garbage can and put it in. Then I go back to where my mother is standing, looking down at the ground where we planted the flowers.

"You go and color now," she says, "and I'll water the flowers."

I go into the house, and take my crayons and coloring book to the table in the Pine Room. This is our family room, where we watch TV and play cards and keep all of the games and toys.

When my mother comes in, she looks down at my picture.

"What's that?"

"It's a house with a blue sky and flowers."

"The blue is wrong. The sky should be lighter." I look down at the drawing. The sky looks good to me. Maybe I can't see it right.

"And the house should be yellow. You should color the house yellow." I was going to make it green, but I'm supposed to make my mother happy, so I pick up the yellow crayon. My mother grabs a broom and goes out onto the porch. She must think I'm not very good at coloring.

The phone rings. I wait for my mother to answer it, but she doesn't seem to hear. I run to the phone and pick up the receiver, answering, "Mayfield residence, Kathy speaking." It's my new friend Susie, asking if I want to come over and play. I like Susie—I have fun playing with her— and I feel excitement climb up my insides. I carefully put the phone down, and go to ask my mother if I can play with Susie. She's sweeping the porch.

"Susie's on the phone. Can I go over to her house and play?" My mother keeps sweeping, back and forth, back and forth, trying to get every speck of dirt off the porch. She's always very careful to keep the house clean and the yard in order.

"After I finish the porch, I'm going to rake some leaves." She stops sweeping and looks down at me, hard. Her big arm muscles tense as she clenches the broom. "Wouldn't you rather help me rake leaves?"

I know I wanted to play with Susie a minute ago, but now I'm not sure. "Susie's on the phone," I repeat. "She wants me to come and play."

My mother is still looking at me, her face tight like it's trying to keep something from escaping, her pointed nose very sharp. "We need to get the leaves raked before your father gets home," she says through the tightness.

Something is surging up inside of me, something I can't stuff down. "But I want to play with Susie," I insist.

My mother turns away and shakes her head. She carefully leans the broom against the porch railing before turning very slowly back to me. "Now, remember what I said? God wants us to cleanse our hearts of angry feelings. You want to go to heaven, don't you?"

Suddenly, I remember what happens to my brother when he doesn't do what my parents want. Now I can't think, and I'm a little afraid. I don't want to whine, or argue, because I'll get in trouble. The only thing left to do is agree. That always keeps me safe. "Okay," I say, as my stomach pulls into itself.

I think about Susie on the phone, waiting, and I decide to just leave the phone there because I don't know how to say no to someone who wants something from me.

As I go to the garage with my mother to get the rakes, dark feelings bubble up to the surface, but I barely notice them before stuffing them back down. I want to do the right thing and make my mother happy, but I want to be happy, too. I can't find a way to do both.

I push the thought out of my mind, and try to think about nothing at all. The hurt goes away somewhere, and I don't feel it any more.

Eventually, I stopped noticing as the hurts piled up. I shut myself down, and I tried to close myself off from the bad feelings that came from my mother, with occasional success. I didn't realize at the time that I was closing myself off from love as well, from the natural ability to connect to others, from life itself.

When I look back on my childhood, what I remember most is a deep sense of isolation, a feeling of being very different from other people.

Lying in bed at night sometimes, holding my bear, I tried to figure out what was wrong. I wanted something from my mother, but I didn't know exactly what it was. I thought there must be a way to fix the problem, but I didn't have any idea how. I wished I could ask someone, but I didn't know who, or what to ask. All I could do was keep trying to make my mother happy, and hope that I would know when I hit the target. All I could do was to be a Good Little Girl. My mother seemed to love the Good Little Girl, and sometimes if I put on the Good Little Girl when she was in a bad mood, she got nice again.

Every morning when I got up, I hoped that I would find a way to fix things so my mother would love me. When the months, and finally years, stretched on without an answer, I decided I must not be worthy of her love and attention.

One night when I was lying in bed, the need for something from my mother got so big that I got up to find her. Padding out into the living room in my footie pjs with a drop seat, I found her sitting on the sofa, watching TV. I knew I wasn't supposed to just run up to her, but I didn't know how to ask for what I wanted. So I just stood there, next to the TV, waiting for her to see me.

My mother didn't notice me. Or, she was ignoring me. So I stepped over to stand in front of the TV, hoping that she would invite me over or come and pick me up.

I felt her eyes stop focusing on the TV, and focus on me instead. She stared at me for a moment.

"You make a better door than you do a window," she grumped.

All of a sudden I knew that the TV was more important than I was. And then I remembered that she didn't talk to me while she was making dinner in the kitchen, so dinner must be more important than I was, too. So many things were more important than I was. As I turned around and went back to bed, I decided I wasn't good enough for my mother to love me.

After that, I didn't try to ask my mother for love. I just gave up. Sadly, I also gave up trying to connect with other people, because at that young age, I just thought it was my fault that no one loved me. I didn't know that other mothers, other people, might be different. I didn't know that love might be possible, even though I knew I wanted it.

I tried with all my child's might to be the Good Little Girl my mother wanted me to be. Along the way, the real me shrank further and further into the background, disappearing bit by bit until I no longer even noticed that I wasn't me anymore. The world around me tilted constantly like a seesaw in a hurricane, depending on my mother's moods, and I scrambled furiously, trying to keep my balance.

Until my mother died, I lived in relentless fear of her anger. The habit of trying to please her, of taking care of her emotionally, became hardwired into my nervous system. Though I toiled endlessly in my attempts to make everything better, the chaos, her anguish, and my sense of myself as a total failure persisted. When I looked inside of myself, there was nothing. I knew I was in there, because I saw things, and I had thoughts, and I could see out. But there was nothing else inside of me, no link to other people or the outside world that I could hold on to. It wasn't until I was in my fifties that I understood the depth of what was missing from my experience of life.

Even after twenty years of digging through the tangle of childhood beliefs to find the gems of truth that allowed me to reconnect with myself, I still work to overcome my sense of isolation, and wrestle with the Good-Little-Girl demons—the shoulds and oughts and society-says-you-have-tos. My struggle has taught me that the road to authenticity is not always easy, but along the way lies treasure:  self-acceptance, self-esteem, and freedom from Good-Little-Girl guilt.

# Chapter 2: Trapped in the Mirror

My parents, Jeroldine and William, grew up during the Depression, and were married in Chicago in 1946. My mother had seven miscarriages before she had me in 1958. It must have been ghastly for her, especially since both of her sisters already had two fine, healthy boys each. Boys were very important in my mother's family.

Our family lived in a pretty house in a typical Midwestern suburb, with tidy flower gardens and jaunty, well-attended bird feeders. The house sat on a lovely piece of property on a dead-end street, with a white picket fence, a huge silver maple in the front yard, and forsythia bushes decorating the end of the driveway. We had three bedrooms and a fireplace, a family room paneled in pine that my mother insisted we call the Pine Room, and a laundry/junk room that we dutifully called the Utility Room. The house was our perfect-family façade: well-built, well-kept, and well-decorated, it was white-shingled with a decorative chimney in the center. It looked like a place where a family could live a happy life, but the phantoms of the bullying and abuse that went on inside the house hid themselves carefully behind the façade of virtue and pious perfection that we presented to the outside world.

After my mother had been through several miscarriages, she and my father adopted my brother. She liked to tell the story: "We brought him here for a weekend visit when he was eighteen months old. And when we got ready to take him back, he cried so much that we decided to keep him."

My brother, Michael, was 7 years old when I was born. I imagine it was hard for him to have had his parents all to himself for so many years, and then suddenly have this tiny, wrinkled thing that his parents called his sister taking up all of his mother's attention, when there wasn't nearly enough love to go around in the first place.

It must have been strange for my mother, after losing all of those possible babies, to have one of her pregnancies result in an actual child. She didn't want to let me out of her sight, and even when I wasn't with her, I could feel her yanking on me, inside, as if I had a Siamese twin who tugged relentlessly in the opposite direction.

My mother always seemed to know where I was and what I was doing. Even when I was an adult, living thousands of miles away, I felt as if there was a TV camera constantly aimed at the back of my head. I thought my mother was psychic, but I suppose most children feel that way. Maybe she just had the same kind of blood-bone-nerves-skin link with me that I felt with her.

In spite of our odd connection, we never really developed an actual mother-child bond. I knew on some level that there wasn't very much love in our family. When my father came home from work, he would stop in the kitchen and kiss my mother on the cheek, which she enjoyed if she wasn't busy, and tried to avoid if she was. That was all the affection I ever saw between my parents, and I never saw any between either of my parents and my brother. I was lucky that I found bits of affection in other places, or I wouldn't have known that love existed.

We had an elderly neighbor, Mrs. Forester, whom I called Fo-Fo because I couldn't quite pronounce her name. Sometimes my mother would leave me with Fo-Fo while she went volunteering, and I knew that Fo-Fo really liked having me there. Her face would light up as soon as she saw me, her voice would get prettier, and she would smile as she reached out to pat my hand. I liked being with Fo-Fo, too, because she would read to me, or talk to me while she cooked. Her rhythm was slow enough that I could think and follow along, and she actually listened to me when I talked.

Once, sitting next to me at her kitchen table, she even taught me to cut out paper dolls with materials she had bought especially for us.

I'm five, and I have a small pair of scissors with rounded ends. I know how to hold them, but I haven't used them very much, only on squares and triangles and circles at school. It seems like a very big job to cut out my first paper doll, and I have to hold it close to my face so I can see what I'm doing.

"See how you can get the scissors to go around her head?" Fo-Fo instructs. "It's almost like a circle. Just follow the way the line of her hair goes with the scissors." I'm really focusing, and I think I'm doing pretty well. "That's good!" she says. "Now follow the line in for her neck, and watch the corner where her shoulder meets it."

I'm going too fast, and I cut into the doll's shoulder a bit. I don't say anything. I'm hoping that Fo-Fo won't notice, because if she does, I'm afraid she'll get mad like my mother does, and make me go away.

"That's okay," she says. "We can put a piece of tape on that. It's hard, the first time, cutting out a paper doll." My chest warms up as if it's smiling.

Fo-Fo was nice and round and cuddly, and sometimes she would put her arm around my shoulders and pull me close to her. I liked that. And she always had cookies for me when I visited. I felt warm and safe and happy with Fo-Fo, and when I visited her, I forgot for a little while how lonely and frightened I felt at home.

When I was six, Fo-Fo fell down her back steps one day, and had to go into a nursing home. My mother took me to visit Fo-Fo a few weeks after she had gone into the home, and she didn't look at all like herself. She was thinner, and her face looked sad. She sat in a wheelchair.

"Hi, Fo-Fo!" I said when we got into her room. I ran over to take her hand. "I missed you!"

"Hello, Kathy," she said. Her eyes didn't sparkle, and she didn't smile.

"How are you doing?"

"Not very well, sweetie."

"I brought my bear. Would you like to see him?"

"Not right now. Thank you for bringing Kathy," she said to my mother.

We didn't stay long. I wished I could make Fo-Fo happy again, but I couldn't. And on the way home I wanted to cry, but my mother usually got angry when I cried, so I pinched my arm instead.

"They should let her eat!" my mother protested, banging her hand against the steering wheel as we were driving home. "She's always loved to eat, and now it's all she has left." She grunted her annoyance, and hit the steering wheel again.

"Why can't she eat?" I asked.

"The doctor put her on a diet because she's overweight," my mother said, her anger spilling over and rasping against me. "But it's killing her. They should just let her eat!" My mother always thought she knew what was best for other people, and sometimes she did. I didn't ask any more questions then, because my mother's angry feelings were already seeping into my skin like tiny bugs.

My mother promised we would go back, but I never saw Fo-Fo again. She died before the end of that year. I wasn't surprised; I was used to my mother breaking promises.

After my mother, cats were the most important personages in our household. We had a scruffy tom named Tony, who enjoyed his monarchy until one day I noticed a beautiful black-and-white cat hanging around the garage. It was late fall, getting chilly, and my mother felt as sorry for her as I did. We started feeding her, and naturally she became part of the family a week or so later. We named her Princess, so I felt a special affinity with her.

It was several weeks before we realized that Princess was pregnant. By then, the temperature was below freezing, and my mother couldn't bring herself to turn Princess out-of-doors, so I had the wonderful experience of watching her give birth to five lovely kittens, which I named Eenie, Meanie, Mynie, Mo, and Dearie. Princess chose my bedroom closet as her maternity ward, and my mother and I sat there late one night, shoulder to shoulder, watching the kittens come into the world by candlelight. It was one of the few times I remember us being on the same track, enjoying our closeness.

We always had cats when I was growing up. They were the only way that members of our family could experience giving and receiving love. We lavished our devotion, our respect and attention on cats. They loved us back unconditionally; they forgave any misdemeanors directed at them almost immediately. My mother and I both appreciated their hedonism, their whimsy, their directness in asking for what they wanted and doing what they pleased. Animals offer and accept love in a way that's very hard for humans to duplicate in their relations with each other, and when I was a child, cats were my only real connection to loving and feeling loved.

But it wasn't always that way. When I was small, I tried to "pass on" the uncomfortable feelings I had about the violence in our family by petting the cats very hard, almost like spanking them. The aftermath of the violence was in my nerves, and my anger wanted to come out *on something*. My body wanted to get rid of it. Kids learn bullying from their parents, and when they're bullied, they seek an outlet for their anger and look for ways to express their own power. I was no exception.

One day, my mother caught me spanking the cat, and for a change, tenderly corrected me. "Gently, gently," she said, and took my hand to show me how to pet a cat gently and smoothly. I really did love our cats; I just needed to let my anger out somehow. After that, I petted gently, and spanked my dolls instead.

Even more than wishing to be a princess, I wished to be a cat, to have the freedom to grow in whatever way I wanted to, the freedom to explore in every direction, to be totally myself.

The day I decided to be a writer, I was six years old. I had written a poem in school, and my teacher proudly had me read it in front of the class. I was so excited to show it to my mother that it felt like there was no air in the world. I thought that finally, finally, I had made something that my mother would like, something she could be proud of me for, something she might love me for. After all, my teacher had liked it, so my mother should, too.

> I feel very important as I open the door and go in.
>
> "Hi, Mommy!" I call as I turn to go in the kitchen, where she usually is when I get home from school. She's standing in front of the cabinet, with the doors open, staring into it. Her narrow face is scrunched up; her pointy elbows stick out as she goes through the cabinet. She pulls out a box of macaroni and cheese, then puts it back.
>
> I try again. "Mommy, I'm home. I have something to show you."

She's still looking in the cupboard. "I don't know," she says. "What am I going to have for dinner tonight?"

My excitement bumps up against my fear of upsetting her. I have to be careful getting her attention, because sometimes it makes her angry. "Mommy," I say, taking the risk, "I wrote a poem in school today."

She pulls out a box of rice. "What?"

"I wrote a poem in school today, and the teacher liked it so much she had me stand up in front of the class and read it. I'm going to be a writer!" My legs want to move, to wiggle and jump with my excitement.

Finally, my mother looks at me. She puts the box down slowly. She has a sad look on her face, and her head wags back and forth, like she's saying no. She asks doubtfully, "Do you think you could do that?" Then she turns back to the cabinet. Suddenly my legs are heavy. Maybe I can't. Maybe the poem wasn't very good after all. I turn away and go to my room, thinking that I'll throw the poem away later.

My mother was always careful to remind me to keep my place, to not stick my neck out, to not try anything new, because I would always fail. But in spite of my constant failure, or perhaps because of it, she exerted continuous effort to make us both alike.

"You're an ice cream lover, just like me," she blurted one night as I was scooping ice cream into a dish.

Getting dinner ready, she took a can of olives from the cabinet. "We both like olives."

After a big meal: "You have a tummy, like mine." She poked hers out further to demonstrate.

Washing dishes together, "Like mother, like daughter."

When I put on my favorite full skirt, "You look better in A-line skirts." That's what she wore.

And out of nowhere, "We're like two peas in a pod."

When I did something she liked: "That's MY daughter!" When I didn't do as well, she ignored me, or criticized me:

"That's not right. Do it this way. No, that's not the way. Here, try this instead. No, you're not doing it right. Well, never mind, just let me do it."

After awhile, I just did things her way. It was so much easier. And deep down, I started believing that doing things her way and acting like her was the only way to get along in the world.

> We're shopping for school supplies.
>
> "You need a new notebook," my mother says. "Pick one out."
>
> I look at the notebooks with their red, yellow, blue, and purple covers, and I want the purple one. Purple is my favorite color.
>
> "How about the red one?" my mother says, as I pull out the purple one.
>
> "I like purple better. It's my favorite color."
>
> "You never told me that," she says, even though I have. "The red one looks better."
>
> I have a choice between getting the color I want and being ignored for the rest of the shopping trip, or taking the red one, making her happy, and feeling a bit sad every time I look at it. The need for peace wins out, and I take the red one. I feel some of her dissatisfaction with her life leap over and land on me. Some of my confidence jumps over to her.
>
> For the rest of the year, whenever I use the red notebook in school, I think of my mother, and wish I had picked the purple one.

Time and time again, she would question my decisions and try to get me to want what she wanted.

"Are you sure you want chicken? *I'm* having shrimp."

"Long hair is harder to take care of. That's why I keep mine short."

"I guess you can wear pants, but *I'm* going to wear a dress."

My mother never wanted to know who I was. She only wanted me to be exactly like her, to want what she wanted. She treated me as if I were only an extension of her, not a person in my own right. And I always felt like an extension, too, as if I wasn't a real person, but only an appendage of my mother's, to be put on or taken off at will. Even though I struggled persistently as an adult to become my own person, to create a comfortable distance between us, I remained an appendage, in both of our minds, until she died at 89.

When I was twelve, my mother suggested I enter a Cook-off Contest for teens sponsored by the local newspaper so I could learn how to cook. I don't know why she suggested the contest, because she didn't like anyone else cooking in her kitchen. Each week, participants would make a recipe printed in the paper, and their families would judge the results on a scale of one to five. I particularly remember the last entry, Cream-Puffs and Eclairs.

> I'm in the kitchen on a Saturday afternoon, assembling the ingredients. My mother stands in the doorway with her hawk-face on, hands fisted on her hips, dark eyes behind their glasses watching every move I make. The recipe suggests starting with the filling first, because it has to set while the dough is made and baked, so I'm mixing the filling in my mother's flowered glazed mixing bowl.
>
> "You should make the dough first," she says, rocking back on her heels so her tummy sticks out even further. "It has to bake before you put the filling in."
>
> I try to pull away from the puppet strings. "The recipe said to make the filling first so it can set."
>
> "Well, I'd make the dough first anyway. Did you preheat the oven?"
>
> "Yes, Mom. I'm supposed to do this myself, you know, with no help from family members."
>
> "I know, I know," she retorts, her thin lips becoming even thinner. "I just thought I could save you from making any mistakes." Thanks, Mom.
>
> I put the bowl of filling in the fridge to set, and start on the dough. My mother's watchful eye makes me nervous, and I spill a bit of flour into the pan while I'm measuring.

"That's too much flour, you've put too much in!" she yaps, pushing her head forward and waving a hand in the air.

"Could you let me do this by myself?"

"Well, I'm sorry I interrupted!" she says in her sing-song voice as she flaps her arms and turns briskly to go into the dining room.

I'm trying to get the dough mixture to form a ball, but with the extra flour, I have to add a little more water. I'm already thinking to myself that it's not going to turn out right.

The dough finally forms a ball. I pull out the cookie sheet and Crisco as I hear my mother call from the living room.

"Don't forget to grease the cookie sheet."

I take in a breath. "I won't." I'm having trouble thinking now. I wish my mother would go find something else to do and leave me alone.

She pops her head in again, smiling, and stands in the doorway watching me as I drop the dough on the cookie sheet by spoonfuls like the recipe suggests.

"Those are too small," she says, still smiling. "There won't be room for the filling."

"Mom, I'm doing what the recipe says. I have to follow their rules!"

"Well, I would make them bigger."

"They're all done now, anyway." I check the oven temp, and carefully place the cookie sheet in the oven. I still have to make the chocolate topping. I get out the double boiler, fill the bottom with water, and put it on the stove.

"Isn't cooking fun?" my mother says. I can't tell whether she's being sarcastic or not.

I want to scream, "NO!", but instead I say, "I guess it is after you've learned how to do it."

I haven't enjoyed myself at any time during the contest. I've done the best I could with each recipe, but I haven't gotten more than a score of three out of five from my family for any dish. I'm hoping the éclairs will net me at least a four, and then, thankfully, the stupid contest will be over.

I got another three. To this day, I still don't enjoy cooking.

Throughout my adult life, I would often hear my mother's voice telling me how to do things, even when she wasn't there. When I went shopping, I felt compelled to hold on to my money until I found a bargain, the way she always did. When I was cooking, I would hear her voice telling me what I was doing wrong. I felt our connection, even halfway across the country, as if some part of me knew what she was thinking, how she was feeling, what she was doing; as if my heart and head were connected to hers by a long, invisible wire.

My mother was always part of me in a physical sense. As a child, I could feel the drifts and gusts of her moods, her thoughts, in my nerves and in my bones. When I reached adulthood, I started noticing my arms and my legs turning into her arms, her legs. She had really good legs, so I'm grateful for that bit of genetic encoding. But it was unnerving to see parts of my body become exact replicas of hers. Not only that, I couldn't fling her out of my psyche. She was all over me, inside and out. Her essence pulsed in every cell in my body. My skin crawled with her. I could not escape her, no matter what I did or where I went. I felt like a fly in a spider web.

When I was a teenager, I decided that I never wanted to be like my mother. But decades later, as I began to unravel the tapestry, I realized that in making that choice, I had left behind my strength, my power, and my intensity—my passion for life. And I discovered then that underneath all of the anger and frustration and disgust, I loved my mother fiercely:  her intensity, her vivacity, her dynamic hunger for excitement and experience. Many times, she was the life of the party. She fought her demons and tried to live a good and moral life. She was tremendously creative, had incredible energy, and was always coming up with new ideas. She grabbed life with both hands and gobbled it up, and then she went looking for more.

In her twenties, she had lived and worked in Chicago, and from the photos I've seen, she was quite a social hit. She was probably the life of the party then as well. But once she married my father in her late twenties, she gave up working and tended to the house, and later, to my brother and me. It must have been difficult for an independent woman to settle down after having seen the world and lived on her own. There was always an undercurrent of dissatisfaction in her behavior, the restlessness of a woman who had tasted the cornucopia of experience the world had to offer, and then left it behind for conventional suburban married life. She found domestic outlets for her wonderful creativity, knitting afghans in bold colors and designs, like red and purple waves or bright orange and brown zigzags; making Christmas ornaments and special cakes; even building a large bookcase out of pine boards and dowel rods for my parents' bedroom. She created many beautiful things over the years, and it always seemed as if she was trying to find herself when she looked for a new craft possibility.

In public, my mother was a lovely, gracious, helpful woman. She volunteered for the local Headstart program, the church, and numerous other organizations throughout her life. Many people saw a very giving and dedicated woman in my mother, and she deeply believed in helping others as much as she could. She was active in the community and involved in women's groups at the church. She read the Bible and struggled valiantly to live by its precepts. But under the surface, she was frustrated and bored—an extremely intelligent and dynamic woman who had few really fulfilling outlets for her energy and creativity.

In later years, her dissatisfaction disintegrated into sadness, and she fought a losing battle with depression in the second half of her life. I echoed her depression because I thought it was part of who I was, just as I believed that all the other things she wanted me to be were part of me. It wasn't until I entered therapy in my thirties that I began to see that we were separate; that she had needed me to be a mirror for her, and that it was too frightening for her to let me be different than she was. But even then, the early training continued to dominate my psyche, and I wasn't able to free myself until she died.

As a child, I tried and tried to reach into her and pull out her real self—I thought it must be in there somewhere. As an adult, I wanted desperately to connect with her, to share the daily ups and downs, to share the depth of human feeling and understanding that our mutually intense experiences of life involved. But something was always in the way.

Even as a child, I sensed my mother's pain, and being born with a healthy dose of compassion, I felt sorry for her and wanted to relieve it. I just didn't know how.

And in spite of being afraid of her, I wanted her love so very much, I knew I would keep trying to get it as long and as hard as I could.

# Chapter 3: The Perfect Family

It's early Sunday morning. There's a slight breeze gliding in the window, and I hear birds happily celebrating their morning meal. My room is cool and quiet, and dark because the blinds are drawn. I drift in and out of sleep and dreams, wanting to snuggle into the warm embrace of my bed for hours.

I hear my mother striding down the hall, and part of me hopes that she'll stop and pat me or give me a kiss good morning, but part of me wants to roll over so my back is to the door. If she's in a hurry, it would be easier that way to hold on to my sense of peace. But I don't roll over, because if she happens to stop by the bed to say good morning, it might look like I'm trying to ignore her, and that would hurt her feelings. Then there might be trouble. So I just stay stuck in the middle, like I always do. That way I don't do anything to upset her.

The door to my room is open. Because I'm only six, I'm not allowed to shut it. Only my mother can shut it, and she only does that when I've done something she doesn't like, and she's sent me to my room.

"Rise and shine!" she calls out in a singsong voice as she bursts into the room to open the blinds. My nerves come right to attention. My mother's presence is palpable as she whirls from window to window, grabbling the cords on the blinds with her gnarled hands and yanking them so they screech to the top of the window. Sunlight floods the room, and I cover my face with the sheet. Having accomplished her mission, she marches out of the room. All of my cells are on alert now; the morning's peace has fled.

Every Sunday, unless one of us was ill, we went to Sunday school and church. We put on our best clothes and our best behavior, and pretended that we were a happy family.

On Sundays especially, we were a unit: the family that prays together stays together. Our religion dictated that we all had to think and feel and do things exactly the same way, as if we were a robot family. I didn't mind going to church, though, because I felt safe there, as if nothing really bad could happen.

Even though we lived in a Grimm's Fairy Tale at home, in public we put on our actors' masks and became a perfect family. We were active members of the Disciples of Christ church, going to Sunday school and service every week, attending the monthly dinners, and even volunteering on Work Days. My parents gave lots of money to the church, and I remember my father sitting at his desk at Christmas, making out checks for donations to the Red Cross and the Salvation Army. A lot of people really liked my parents, and thought they were wonderful. They were gracious and kind, always ready to help anyone outside of our family, and they did a lot of volunteer work over the years. We even had children from the orphanage come and visit for a weekend once or twice a year, to help us see that we were better off than some other children were, to help us learn compassion, and to give them a nice weekend with a loving family.

One time, we welcomed a girl named Elizabeth, who was exactly my age, six years old. She was a real sweetheart, and my mother took a great liking to her.

> Elizabeth and I sit at the dining room table after Sunday dinner, coloring in some of my coloring books. I'm using the green-blue crayon, and she wants it.
>
> "Where's the green-blue?" she asks. "I want to color some water."
>
> "I'm using it," I tell her. "I'll be done in a moment, and then you can have it." That seems reasonable to me.
>
> My mother calls from the kitchen, "Kathy, give her the crayon. She's our guest." My mother has been making me give Elizabeth my dolls, my toys, even my clothes. Yesterday, my mother went through my wardrobe and picked out some

blouses that she thought Elizabeth might want to take with her when she goes back to the orphanage. One of them was my favorite, a pink blouse with lace at the collar, which always made me feel pretty when I wore it.

I know I'm supposed to feel sorry for Elizabeth, but I want to fling the crayon at her and run to my room to keep the rest of my stuff safe. I'm stuck between my feelings and what I know I'm supposed to do. My mother always lets other people have what they want, but not me. My lower lip wants to stick out, my arms want to hit things. But I don't want to make my mother angry, so I give Elizabeth the crayon instead.

"Here," I say, pushing it at her. I pick up the orange crayon, even though I don't know what I want to draw with it. My need to fling the crayon goes somewhere and hides.

Later, when we were driving Elizabeth back to the orphanage, my mother went on and on about how much she had enjoyed the weekend.

"It's been lovely to have you, Elizabeth! You're such a nice little girl, and you're so pretty." My mother's voice seems to caress Elizabeth, to stroke her with love and admiration. "You have such beautiful hair. I really enjoyed brushing it." Elizabeth's hair was blond; mine was brown. Suddenly I felt ashamed of my shiny brown hair. "I hope you like your new clothes, and I hope you visit again soon!" As we dropped Elizabeth off, my mother gave her a big hug and petted her hair one last time. I was afraid my mother would decide at the last minute to take Elizabeth back home and leave me at the orphanage, but it didn't happen. I felt lucky that time.

My parents left a real legacy of giving. Offering their time, talent, and treasure was one of the primary values they espoused, and many people's lives were made better by their generosity. They helped out at the church, and after my father retired, they both volunteered a lot of their time to various organizations. I found their behavior confusing, because they had this huge public image of goodness, but there was so much darkness and pain—what Jung would have called the "shadow"—in the privacy of our home. It was like being in two movies at once, and I had to try to keep up with the plot line as best I could, ready to switch into the public character at a moment's notice whenever the doorbell rang.

The church was a big part of our lives, providing lists of rules and regulations to live by, like "Do what the Bible says," "Turn the other cheek," "Give up the things you want and focus on helping others." But the reasons behind the rules were never explained. The mystery of spiritual experience was missing; the dogma was didactic. There was no larger connection to the thread of life. Instead, we were insular, isolated from the fullness of life by the necessity of having to live by the precepts of the church. Religion gave my parents comfort amidst the uncertainty of life, and offered a preordained set of values to live by, so that difficult choices didn't have to be made.

My father's father was a minister, and his father had been a minister before him. When my father finished high school, my grandfather suggested he carry on the family tradition and go into the ministry. But my father told him in no uncertain terms that he would never become a minister because he didn't want to do to his family what his father did to theirs. Still, we carried on the tradition of fervent devotion.

"Bless this food to our use, and bless the hands that prepared it." This standard line from the blessing my father always gave before we ate made me imagine the light of God coming down on my mother's hands as a blessing for her labor in preparing the meal. The funny thing was that my mother's rheumatoid arthritis was so bad that her fingers were gnarled, the joints so big she had to stop wearing her wedding rings. She lived with a lot of pain from those blessed hands. But she never let that pain hold her back.

Even when we went to a restaurant, we each bowed our heads and said a silent blessing when the food arrived. We prayed as we sat in the car before leaving home, and I was taught to say prayers before I went to bed. My parents never explained the reasoning behind all the praying, and it wasn't until I was well into adulthood that I began to understand the philosophy of offering gratitude for life's gifts, of connecting with a greater universal force. When I was a child, it was just another rule we had to follow, devoid of any genuine sense of meaning.

The Sunday morning goal was to leave by exactly 8:40 am. If we were a minute or two late getting in the car, my mother got terribly anxious.

"Hurry up! We don't want to be late to church," she would say, her voice getting higher and louder as she tried to herd us out the front door. She would issue orders: "Kathy, hurry up, get your coat. Michael, don't forget to put on a tie." For years, I thought that being late to church was an unforgivable sin. If we were running late, my mother's movements would get fast and jerky, as if she could hurry us along by moving faster herself. The faster she moved, the more I wanted to slow things down so I could process what was going on, and then she would say, "Don't dawdle." So I'd move back into her rhythm, start hurrying, and shove everything else into the back of my mind to process later. I didn't get to it all until I was in my thirties and forties.

This morning my mother is all decked out in a crisp blue blouse and blue skirt with huge red and yellow flowers. My father and my brother are in stiff suits, looking uncomfortable. My mother looks gay in comparison, with the vivid flowers and her bright red lipstick; she enjoys going to church because it's a very social event for her. I'm eight years old, and I'm dressed in a light green cotton dress with a zipper up the front.

Dressing myself is always tricky, because I never know whether what I've chosen will satisfy my mother. This morning, I put on my white blouse and red jumper, which I've worn countless times to church. But when I walk into the dining room, my mother pins me with her gaze and says, "You're not wearing that, are you?" Her voice is sharp and disapproving, and I feel stupid. There must be something wrong with it that I can't see, like a stain or a tear. I look carefully, but I don't see anything. I'm at a loss. Why doesn't she like it this time?

"What's the matter with it?" I ask.

She doesn't answer me. Instead, she says, "Why don't you wear your green dress with the zipper?" So I go back to my room to change, without knowing why.

Some days, when I didn't have the fortitude to face the routine of criticism, I would ask my mother, "What should I wear today?" Most of the time, she would answer huffily, "Whatever you want. You don't have to ask me. You're too old for that." But I knew that whatever I chose, she would probably find something wrong with it. Her inconsistency made my brain feel squishy.

I never found a place in the middle where I didn't have to ask and she didn't criticize. It was like trying to learn a dance routine in which the arrangement of the steps changed constantly without warning. And when she didn't criticize me, I would wonder what I did right, and whether I could do it again, or whether she thought I was hopeless, not worth her attention at all. Over the years, the experience of never being sure of where I stood taught me to question every decision I made.

The Christian Church we went to was well-appointed: a lovely brick building with a gorgeous sanctuary, lots of rooms for Sunday school classes, beautifully framed religious pictures on the walls, and a huge square bell tower with small windows that looked like the watchtower from a medieval fortress. The grounds were beautifully landscaped, a testimony to the wealth of the church. The church did a lot of good for the community, and the people at church were always polite, always willing to offer a helping hand, just like my parents.

The church was surrounded on three sides by a country club golf course, and sometimes when we drove into the parking lot, we saw people riding in golf carts or teeing off. I always wanted to go over and see how people lived at the country club. I thought it would probably be much more fun than church. It was like another whole world that we never got to visit—a world that offered glimpses of ease and luxury and enjoyment and peace—and I wondered if there was more life and love on the other side of that fence. But my parents always frowned when they saw the people over there, as if those were the people that were going to Hell when we went to Heaven.

Sunday school started at 9:00. Most of the time I didn't mind Sunday school. There were books, which I loved, and sometimes there were games. Sometimes we got to play characters in the Bible. But the Bible stories, with their messages of guilt and shame, were pounded into our heads over and over. I still cringe when I hear the song "Jesus Loves Me," especially the line about "We are weak but He is strong." I imagine that line is responsible for more cases of low self-esteem than any other childhood ditty.

In my younger years, the Sunday school teachers read Bible stories to us from books with heavenly illustrations of places and animals. In later years, we read from them ourselves and did Bible word games, and crafts, like pouring papier-mâché into aluminum pans, placing shells in the goop, and letting them dry to make awkward and extremely breakable paper weights, or making crosses out of sticks and brightly colored yarn that dogs loved to gnaw on when people took the crosses home.

Between Sunday school and the church service, my mother gaily chats with other church members, while my father sits in the car and smokes. He's not much of a "people person" the way my mother is. He has a very hard time joining in any kind of social activity.

I'm with my mother in the Friendship Room, a large beige conference room with a stage at one end. My mother is giving her opinion on the Sunday school lecture to some of her friends. Her face is bright, her gestures animated, and everyone in the group is looking at her as if they're quite entertained. She can be very entertaining when she wants to be, and even downright funny if she's in a humorous mood. She has the group's attention, and I'm standing a little beside and behind her, like a forgotten doll.

I feel like I have to be on my guard here because there are too many people standing around talking too loudly and smiling too broadly, some of the women are wearing too much makeup, and the men look like Ken dolls in their Sunday suits and ties. Everyone has a plastic veneer over them, as if their real selves and their real lives are hidden away for the day, and they're all trying to be very polite and make points so they can get into Heaven. I don't know what to make of all that, so I just put on a plastic veneer, too, and my best fake Sunday smile like an actor in a play.

Everyone speaks the same language at church. It's very limited. It doesn't include any words that describe emotion. I'm familiar with that because it's just like my family. All references to any kind of personal spiritual experiences are filtered through the warped and dusty lens of Bible references. Most of the time, people just make polite chitchat, and since I'm about half as tall as most of the adults, the chatter around me quickly turns into a drone of painted faces and size extra-large smiles pasted over neckties tied too tight, and I drift into the inside of my head. I imagine the thoughts that people have underneath what they're saying zinging back and forth across the room above their heads. I can feel those real thoughts in my nerves, and they make me jumpy. I don't know exactly what they mean, but they don't match the conversation, and I wonder why those thoughts don't come out of people's mouths instead of all the polite chitchat. I know that in my family, we try to turn off our real thoughts when we put on a dress—or in the case of my dad and my brother, a suit—but I can never get my real thoughts to stop, so mostly I keep my mouth closed so no real thoughts escape.

There are lots of things I can't say because of our church language limitations. If someone asks me how I'm doing, I can't say, "I fell down this morning and skinned my knee and I got blood all over my new dress, so Mommy got mad and said a bad word, and then I had to change my dress and we were late because Mommy had to wash my knee and put that stuff on it that really stings, and some Band-aids, and then Daddy drove too fast because we were late, and when we got stopped by a big, mad policeman, Daddy said a bad word, too...."

Instead, I have to say, "Fine." I can't ever tell other people what's really going on or how I really feel. I can't tell them about the Russells next door, who scream at their kids, or about my mother getting angry and banging all the pots and pans around in the kitchen sometimes when she's making dinner, or about the bruises my brother has under his clothes. I don't think God would like people doing those kinds of things, and if I told, He might send them to Hell. So I can't tell people how awful things are at home or how scared I am there. Even if I did tell them, no one would believe me because my parents are so nice to them. The only things I can say to adults are really safe things like, "Those are pretty flowers on your dress," or "That's a nice tie," even when I know that the man I'm saying this to is just dying to take off his tie and loosen his collar.

When we stand in a large group, all I can see without looking up are belts and bosoms. There are some humongous bosoms, and one of the larger ones, belonging to a woman dressed in huge polyester flowers, Mrs. Briggs, notices that I'm not involved in the conversation. She leans down, her bracelets clanging, in a vaporous cloud of powder and sweet perfume that makes me want to sneeze.

"I REALLY ENJOYED the piano pieces you played at the last dinner," she gushes. "Your mother must be so PROUD." If she is, she's never told me. I know she enjoys the attention she gets from other people when I play. But that doesn't seem to be the same as being proud of me.

The necklace on Mrs. Briggs' bosom dangles inches from my nose as the straining flowers dance in front of my face, and I try not to sneeze. "WHEN are you going to play another LOVELY CONCERT?" The people in the group turn my way, smile and nod as they look down at me, and murmur their appreciation as well. And suddenly my mother turns, too, noticing there is more attention to be had where I am. She puts her hands on my shoulders, and stands up taller, as if she truly is proud of me.

"She's been playing since she was four," she informs them. "We had to start her with fifteen-minute lessons, because she could only sit still for fifteen minutes at a time." My polite smile turns into a mile-wide grimace that threatens to break my face, and I feel icky and pleased all at the same time. There's a gentle, invisible pressure from my mother's hands moving me inch by inch to the side again, signaling that my ten seconds of being in the spotlight are over. I can feel her gobbling up the attention I got.

My mother played the piano, too, and she played very well. We even played duets sometimes, but it didn't feel like fun, it always felt like my mother had to be the best. Her arthritic knuckles caused her to miss notes sometimes, and I felt like I had to make little mistakes so I wouldn't seem better than she was. It was only years later, when my mother began sharing confidences with me about her own childhood that I began to understand why everything between us seemed like a competition.

I often felt I was only a prop in my mother's life, to be pulled out like a hat or a book when she was in the mood, to be used to obtain whatever she needed in the moment. I couldn't be assertive, I couldn't be too creative, I couldn't be too smart or social or organized, or I'd tempt more competition. I was supposed to disappear until I was wanted. I was expected to be a Good Little Girl, to be 100% polite 100% of the time.

My favorite thing at church is going to the bathroom. It's clean and quiet and beautiful inside, everyone respects your space, and the women speak in hushed tones, like in a library. They probably call it the Ladies' Room because everyone acts like a lady in there. Everything is tiled in soft shades of green, and we have to speak softly, or our voices will sound harsh and loud bouncing off the tile. Pretty silk flowers in a beautiful vase smile at me from a small table, like an altar. There are a lot of windows up by the high ceiling, and the light is soft and beautiful, like I imagine it is in Heaven. I feel like God is in the bathroom, and I think that's funny, because I don't feel him anywhere else in the church.

When we're in the bathroom, my mother's attention is actually focused on me in a nice way. She's a real Lady. She asks me politely and quietly if I'm done, and she waits patiently for me to finish washing and drying my hands.

Years later, my mother told me that when we were in public bathrooms, I would wash and wash and wash my hands, and dry them over and over, and I think it was because it was the only time she waited for me. The rest of the time, I had to move at her tempo, whether I was ready to or not. I was like a real person in the church's bathroom, somebody worthy of attention. I felt very clean in there, and almost honored to be in such a beautiful place.

After Sunday School and the social inter-mission, we head over to church. It's slow going: on the way my mother likes to stop and chat a moment with everyone she knows. Her voice lilts up and down, and my attention wanders to the sights and sounds around me.

Everything is glass and marble and beige, with little plants and religious pictures perfectly spaced along the entrance hall to the sanctuary. I feel as if I should be wearing long robes here instead of my green cotton dress with the zipper up the front.

I pass the time while I wait for my mother by looking at the huge book that lists the names of people who have given memorial donations: the silk curtains in the walkway given by a daughter in memory of a father, the paintings in the chancel given by a family in memory of grandparents, etc. I wonder what their families are like: whether every family is like mine when they're at home, or whether some of them are different, maybe even fun. Do they get mad at each other a lot like my family does, or are they really and truly nice, like some of the people at church seem to be?

There is glory, beauty, peace, and love in church, but we never take any of it home with us.

The sanctuary is huge, with a cream-colored marble altar the size of a large sofa, tall gold candlesticks, and beautiful golden lights hanging down from the ceiling. There are vases of lovely, nodding flowers on the altar and on the steps, given by someone in the congregation in memory of someone, as noted in the Sunday bulletin. I want to run my fingers over the fancy carvings on the wooden pews, but I know that's wrong. It's a sin to do anything my mother wouldn't like. The steps are covered with soft red carpet that looks like velvet. With the cream and red and gold, the high ceilings, the magnificent wood paneling and lovely stained glass windows, and everyone speaking in lowered voices, it feels like I'm in a rich person's castle. I feel even more like the Poor Little Match Girl in the church than I do at home.

Behind the altar is a huge cross, lest we should forget that someone went through a lot of pain because of our sins.

I was midway into my adult life before I realized that what I thought were "sins" as a child were mostly mistakes I made because I didn't know better, like asking my mother why someone's ankles were lumpy, or putting dishes away in the wrong place, or forgetting my homework when I left for school. Some of the "sins" were just things my parents taught me were bad, like saying what I felt, or getting angry about something somebody did to hurt me. My parents weren't very good at teaching us about life, about how to handle the ups and downs or make good decisions or create mutually respectful and fulfilling relationships, but they excelled in teaching us rules and enforcing them.

"Get your elbows off the table!"

"Don't talk with your mouth full." That rule was hard to follow when someone asked me a question.

"Ask to be excused before you leave the table."

"Don't make any noise in church." That made me want to ask, "You mean I can't sing the hymns or join in the prayers?" But my mother would have thought I was making a smart remark, and then she'd threaten to wash my mouth out with soap.

> The service begins at 10:25 with an organ prelude, graceful music that makes me forget all about the rules and the problems, and lets me just drift in the beauty of the sound and the lush surroundings. The music sounds like God is singing, but the rest of the service doesn't make sense to me. It just feels like words and rules, and when I listen to the feelings in the room, everyone seems to be bound by invisible ropes. I don't feel God there at all, except when the music is playing.
>
> At 10:30 the music stops, and the bell tolls solemnly, reminding me to pay attention. The sanctuary smells of flowers and candle wax and polished wood. The minister strides to the podium, all power and authority in his black velvet robes, ready to tell us what we're doing wrong. In a commanding voice, he opens with a long prayer while we all close our eyes and bow our heads and try not to fall asleep, and then he begins the service, which seems to go on and on, the tedium broken only by the choir's singing, when I can again float and drift on beautiful music.
>
> The sermon is the worst: I get so bored that I add up all the numbers posted on the hymn boards at the front of the church. I add them up vertically, horizontally, and diagonally to see whether any of the totals match. I look at the backs of other people's necks, the ones who sit in the pews in front of us, and I compare an old

man's neck to a young man's, memorize what a heavy necklace looks like digging into the back of a woman's neck, and wonder about hairlines on the backs of necks. It's one of the few places on their own body a person can't see, so it seems kind of secret and revealing, all at the same time, as if it might expose the hidden side of someone's personality. The back of an older man's neck is often pudgy and wrinkled, even if he's thin. The young men's necks are straight and strong. The heavy necklace a woman wears makes her skin bunch up around it, and I wonder if it hurts.

When I get really bored, I play with my fingers, touching each one to every other one, as if somehow when I finish, the Universe will come to order. If I forget to sit still and start to swing my feet, my mother places a gentle hand on my knee, and I know to stop immediately, or "suffer the consequences," which is her way of saying "Look out!" She's never explained what "consequences" means, so I always obey the rules. It's the only way I know to keep myself safe.

Sometimes my mother takes notes on the bulletin during the sermon, so she can comment on it later. My brother, Michael, is sitting sullenly on the other side of my mother, looking at his hands in his lap. I wonder what he thinks, how he passes the time in church. We don't really know each other, because he's seven years older than I am, and because my mother is always in between us, even when she isn't there.

My father falls asleep sometimes during the sermon. His head begins to dip, then jerk back up, then dip again and jerk back up a few times until his chin comes to rest gently on his bow tie. I enjoy watching the process out of the corner of my eye, and at a certain time of year, the sun is just touching his thinning hair, the colors of the stained-glass window shining through the meager places and making all the hairs seem to vibrate with light, like the halo that Jesus has in all the paintings.

My father's narcolepsy happened more and more often as he got older. It wouldn't have been a problem, except that he snored, so my mother would gently place her hand over his and squeeze it or wiggle it a little until he woke up. In church, she was gentler with us than she was at any other time, maybe because she didn't want to disturb the service, or because we were in public. As an adult I often wondered if my father developed the habit of falling asleep so he could have some peace whenever he wanted it, in the midst of a guilt-producing sermon or during a boring conversation when company came over.

I didn't begrudge him the peace he might have found, because sometimes monsters came out of the walls at home and took him over.

# Chapter 4: The Monsters

I'm four years old. I'm in my room, playing with my dolls, and I hear a funny sound coming from my brother's room down the hall—like a plastic ball hitting a racket. Thwack! Thwack! I think maybe he's got a new game, or he's building something, because the sound happens over and over, like when my father is hammering something, but not as loud.

But somehow it doesn't feel like a game, in my nerves; it feels like there's a monster in the house. I get up and creep down the hall to peek in. Sometimes my brother doesn't like me interrupting him, so I have to be careful to check first. He's lying on his bed with the blue bedspread on it, face down, and my father has a belt in his hand. He's raising it up in the air, and bringing it down on my brother over and over again. That's what the sound is. I can't see Michael's face, and he's not making any noise. My father's face is contorted so that he looks like a monster. This isn't the nice daddy I know who asks other people what they would like to do or goes along with whatever my mother wants or gives money to the church or builds things for me like stilts and a playhouse. This isn't my daddy. I don't know who it is. It must be a monster that got inside him somehow.

I back away and run down the hall to my room. I jump into my bed and hug my bear, curling up tightly into a little ball. I think my father is going to kill my brother, and I don't know what to do about it. All I can do is hide and be good and hope that the monsters won't come and get me, too.

Forever after that, I worried that if I didn't do what my parents wanted, or if I upset them in any way, I would be killed.

I don't remember how often my father hit Michael, but at the time it seemed to happen regularly. At eleven, Michael was tall for his age, but his shoulders were hunched, and he skulked around the house like a shadow in a movie. He had dark brown hair and a cocky smile that tried to hide the pain in his eyes. He never made a sound when my father beat him, and never talked about it. He just started staying away from home more and more, coming home later and later. Sometimes he ran away, and my parents would get a phone call at night from the police.

"Your son is here. Please come and pick him up." Many times my parents made the trip to pick him up. Once, when he was a little older, he got as far away as Springfield, 200 miles away. Finally, my parents stopped making the trips. I never knew how Michael managed to get home again.

I imagine that running away was his way of letting everyone know that there were BIG PROBLEMS in our family. But my parents never considered finding out what the real issue was, they just labeled my brother "bad." And though I often wanted to get away from my parents, too, I saw what happened when Michael ran away, so I never tried to leave. After awhile, the wanting to get away went so deep inside of me, I forgot I wanted to, and just learned to live in the chamber of fear.

Michael and I didn't talk much. The space between us was huge, and I never knew who he was. Sometimes I wish that, when I was small, someone had pointed out that it was the dysfunction in our family that caused my parents to label him "bad." They needed a scapegoat to maintain their belief in their own goodness. For me, it was much less threatening to cover everything up and fudge about whether things bothered me, to be phony instead of straightforward. Unfortunately, that became part of my basic beingness in the world until my parents died. I just abandoned myself and became my parents' version of what a child is supposed to be like.

It wasn't just the threat of annoying my mother or being punished, it was that the threat of God's wrath hovered all the time, too. I could never figure out where the line was that we couldn't cross without incurring the wrath of God, or why He was merciful to some people and mean to others. Nobody ever made that quite clear. So I just followed whatever rules were in force at the time, living in survival mode so I could be safe.

But Michael stood strong in the midst of it all. He said what he truly thought in spite of the threat of punishment, and as an adult, I respect that. I didn't start having opinions on anything until I was in my forties, because I didn't really have many thoughts of my own. I simply did what I was told. I was unaware that I was unaware.

My brother only grew up thinking he was bad because that's the picture my parents gave him to live, the projection of things they couldn't bear to think might be inside themselves. I don't think that's really who he is. It seems to me that he's actually a good guy with a good heart. He just got messed up by my parents.

Sometimes, at the dinner table, Michael would make what my parents called a smart remark, and then flinch away from my father in case he got slapped. But my father never hit him at the dinner table; he was too polite.

"Angie says Greg is having trouble in school." My mother liked to talk about the neighbors, especially when they were having problems.

Michael tried to join in the conversation. "That's no surprise. Greg doesn't do his homework. And he's not very smart." And then he would flinch, because my parents preferred to be the only ones who judged someone else, and he was afraid my father would hit him for voicing his opinion.

My mother needed so much of the attention so much of the time that the only space of real attention Michael could find was the one where he did and said things my parents didn't like. The only way he could get any importance in the family was by being bad. My mother took up all the rest of the importance.

Sometimes my father would compliment the meal my mother had made, and Michael would blurt out the truth, the same way my mother sometimes did. "Well, except that the meat is a little overdone," he would say. That got my mother's attention, and she would bristle. Unfortunately, the ways in which Michael tried to mirror my parents' behaviors didn't meet with their approval.

A lot of Michael's "smart remarks" were actually the truth. He was the only one in the family who pointed out what was really going on, the only one besides my mother who actually said what he felt. He was the truth-teller. I usually said whatever I thought my parents wanted me to say so that I could be safe, and because doing so usually made the tension level go down.

"I think the meat is good. I like it well done," I would say as it soaked up every last drop of saliva in my mouth, and my mother's bristles would diminish.

I was constantly confused by all the talk about being good that was mixed in with the lying and phoniness, but I imagine that happens a lot in super-religious families. Sometimes I wonder if my brother could see through it all because his DNA was different. Or maybe he was just smarter than I was.

My father was very passive around my mother, and often deferred to her decisions. Even if my mother asked for his opinion, he would say, "Well, I don't know, honey, whatever you want to do is fine." I imagine it was just easier for my father to go along with what my mother wanted, like it was for me. When we asked him what he preferred, he always said, "I don't have any druthers." Maybe his druthers disappeared early in their married life when he figured out that the marriage wasn't going to turn out exactly like he had hoped.

My mother mentioned once that when my father asked her to marry him, she said, "Don't let me run the household the way my mother did." But apparently my parents' early psychological imprinting was at least as strong as mine.

Except for the way he treated my brother, my father was the nicest guy you could ever meet. He was kind and gentle, with a good heart and good intentions. If someone needed something and he could help in any way, he would lend as many hands as he could. He was an exceptional role model for taking other people's needs into consideration, and trying to live for the good of all. I learned a lot from him. He was the model for my Good Little Girl behavior, and his actions throughout his life deeply shaped my perceptions of what it means to be a kind and compassionate human being.

If it's true that people get points toward Heaven when they do good things, I'm sure he had a lot when he got there. But when he took the belt to Michael, he was like a raging maniac, and that was frightening and confusing. It taught me that people could turn on a dime and become monsters at a moment's notice if I didn't do what they wanted. That's how I became a doormat.

Michael was a very talented artist. He could render a still life, a bird, or a person in a beautiful and vividly realistic drawing. He worked alternately in pencil and in chalk, and his artwork always received very appreciative comments.

I loved Michael's pictures. When I was about five, he drew a gorgeous picture of a cardinal, artfully detailed in a lovely, perfect shade of red. My mother, a huge fan of cardinals, placed it on a large bulletin board in the hallway that connected the bedrooms. When I stood in front of it, it hung just above my head. I can still remember the vaguely sweet smell of the chalk, and the very soft and fuzzy look of the cardinal.

I'm curious about what the cardinal feels like, so I put my finger on it and rub the softness. It feels just as silky as I thought it would feel, and it feels really good to rub it. As I'm rubbing, the chalk smears past the outline of the bird's body. No other picture I have ever touched has smeared like that. I feel really bad, because it's such a beautiful picture, and I start to get frightened about what my mother always calls "the consequences."

When my mother sees what I've done, her words make my fear bigger.

"That was not a nice thing to do." She sounds like the minister in the church. "We're going to have to punish you."

"I didn't mean to," I cry out. "It smeared when I rubbed it. I'm sorry." I'm shaking now. But my mother will not be moved.

I'm so frightened, I almost wet my pants. I'm afraid my father is going to hit me with the belt like he hits Michael. Even though I know I'm not supposed to cry, the tears come gushing out as I shake, and I keep saying, "I'm sorry!" My mother takes me to my room and sits me down on the bed.

"You wait here," she says. She goes down to the basement to talk with my father, who is in his workshop, and a few moments later she appears in the doorway to my room with my father behind her. "Go with your father," she says. "And I'll try to fix the picture."

I look at my father. His head seems to be trying to disappear into his neck, and his lips look pouty. My mother always seems so huge and pushy and sharp in contrast to my father, who often seems to be trying to become invisible.

He takes me to the Utility Room, the room with the heating system and washer and dryer and assorted junk.

I repeat my pleas to my father, much louder this time.

"No, daddy, please! I didn't mean to! I won't do it again! I'm sorry!" He doesn't say anything. The boxes of junk in the room suddenly seemed huge, and the one window in the room looks out on the bleakness of winter. My father picks up a stack of papers from an old, rickety chair, and puts them on the washing machine. Then he takes my hand, pulls me gently over to him, turns me over his knee, and gives me a couple of half-hearted spanks before helping me up.

I was amazed and relieved that it didn't hurt much. But it hurt my dignity, and strengthened my resolve to disappear the impulses of my real self, and to try harder to be the Good Little Girl at all times. Finally, I just adopted the Good Little Girl persona for everything, and gave up my real self. It was easier that way.

My father made only occasional references to his early life.

"I used to like to go to the Saturday night dance, and stand below the platform watching people's feet as they danced," he said once. "All of a sudden, my father would be behind me saying, 'William. Don't you think it's time to come home.'"

He never even tried to dance—he was only watching—and he still got in trouble. He had to be perfect, because his father was the village minister. I wonder sometimes if he was getting back at his father when he punished my brother.

Every year my parents would go to the New Year's Eve Dance that my father's company held, a fancy dress-up affair with exquisite food in a beautiful hotel ballroom. My mother loved to dance. My father, always uncomfortable at social events, got even more itchy when called upon to dance, but he wanted very badly to please my mother. Decades later, when he was in his nineties and suffering from dementia, he often said that he should have taken my mother dancing more often, punishing himself with the guilt of not having done better, and hoping that if he punished himself enough, God or my mother wouldn't do it when he got to Heaven.

My father was an excellent amateur photographer. He had several expensive cameras, which he bought used at a good price. He always took pictures: at family events, on outings and vacations, and at Christmas as we opened our presents. It was as if he were recording images of other people living because he couldn't jump in and participate himself.

He had a workshop in the basement where he made things like stilts and a playhouse for me, and bookshelves for Michael. He loved to make things. If anyone needed something, he could make it.

All the nuts and bolts and nails and screws in his workshop were sorted into little jars, and each tool had its place on his workbench, as if by ordering his workshop, he could make some sense of his life.

His workshop was the place he kept his creativity and his confidence and his sense of self. It's the place he escaped to in the middle of an argument with my mother, when he knew he wasn't going to win—which was always. It was the only place where he could be who he truly was, the one place where he had complete control.

One day when I was eight, my father taught me how to hammer and saw.

> The smell of sawdust is strong down here, making the workshop feel fresh and clean. "Hold the nail straight up and down, don't let it tilt," he directs. "That's right. Now be really careful the first few times you hammer it, so you get it set the right way." I have a small silver-colored hammer in my hand, and I want to do it just right to please him. It's hard to hold the nail steady with one

hand while I'm swinging the hammer with my other hand.

"Watch your fingers, you don't want to hurt yourself. Careful—hold the nail straight up and down. That's right." I'm so proud that I can get the nail to stay in the board, and it's pretty straight. But I can't show that I'm proud, because that would be a sin. So I just bury the pride deep inside where I won't find it for a long, long time, and go on to the next task, sawing a small board.

I'm in between the sawhorses, holding the board with my left hand and the saw with my right. He stands on the other side of the sawhorse on my right, holding that end of the board to keep it steady. He's totally focused on my work. "You have to move the saw in a straight line, you can't let it wiggle back and forth. That's right. Keep going, it takes a little elbow grease." Sawing is even harder than nailing. I can't figure out how to keep the saw going straight in and out, but I manage to saw the board in two. The pride doesn't even surface this time. I've learned my lesson well.

I want to ask him for something, something that would fill an empty place inside me, but I don't know what it is or how to ask.

"Now go upstairs and get ready for dinner," he says as he turns back to his workbench.

I went upstairs, understanding a bit of the comfort my father felt being in his workshop. The pace was slower than it was around my mother; I had time to process things and I could sense space around me, not the tautness that seemed to close in on me when my mother was in the room. There was a sense of possibility, an invitation to create new things out of what was there.

When I was small, I felt as if my father truly cared for me, but in retrospect our relationship seems very dry. Neither of my parents knew how to express affection, and when I was an adult,

I was the first to say, "I love you" to them. It was almost a year before they could say it back to me.

When my father made the occasional slip-up that called for a Band-aid, he would come to me. It started about the time I was old enough to manage unwrapping a Band-aid, maybe six.

"I cut my finger. Will you put a Band-aid on it?"

"Ouch," I would say. Or, "That looks like it hurts. I hope it gets better." In later years, he continued to show me his cuts and bruises and sore thumbs and ingrown toenails and varicose veins and funny-looking moles, and it felt stranger and stranger the older I got, as if I was more like a mother than a daughter, as if I should kiss his injuries and make them better. The responsibility for making his life worthwhile, for making him feel loved, fell on my shoulders, because he didn't get much attention from my mother. I always felt I had to pay attention to him when he needed it, to get him included somehow in what was going on, because my mother just moved on ahead whether anyone was coming along with her or not.

One of his hobbies was drawing graphs of the progress of his mutual funds in relation to the stock market. He spent most of his spare time doing that, when he wasn't making things in his workshop, and he often showed me his work. My mother didn't want anything to do with his investing. When I became an adult and went to visit, he'd talk for an hour or more about his investments while I'd sit listening to his monologue, bored to tears. I sensed his loneliness, and I felt sorry for him, so for almost twenty years I sat time after time, visit after visit, looking at his graphs and listening to what he had to say about the stock market. In spite of my boredom, I learned a lot about investing. He was a good provider, and a good investor. He knew what he was doing.

In the late 1990s, I showed my father how to create one of his graphs on the computer, but he would have none of it. It had to be done his way—by hand—or it was worthless. He was fascinated by the Internet at first, but then it got too big for him, and he started saying, "The Internet is a bunch of hoo-haa."

As he got older, he spent more and more time in the basement, and less time interacting with people. My need to include him became insatiable. It may have helped me to feel like everything was more balanced when I included him, and it probably protected me from feeling like I was becoming my mother. I imagine it also kept me from facing my own feelings of loneliness and lack of emotional connection with other people.

My need to include my father didn't sit very well with my mother.

> I'm an adult now, visiting my parents for Christmas. My mother and I are finishing the dishes in her pink kitchen. The smell of liver and onions lingers in the air. She really dislikes liver, but she makes it occasionally for dinner because my dad and I enjoy it. She wipes the dishes with energy and enthusiasm. She's in one of her good moods, and I know I'd better enjoy it while I can.
>
> "Want to play cards?" she asks. She loves to play cards.
>
> "Sure." I like playing cards, too. It's one of the few times we have a little fun.
>
> "What do you want to play?"
>
> My need to include my father bumps up against my need to keep my mother happy. She's already in a pretty good mood, so he wins this time.
>
> "Well, if we play rummy, we can ask Dad to play." Her enthusiasm wanes a little.
>
> "Okay. Why don't you ask him?"

Playing cards made my father feel guilty, the way dancing did, but I assumed that feeling left out must have made him feel worse, so I always suggested that we ask him to play. My mother would rather have a fast and furious game of double solitaire at which I would lose, because she loves to win. Even when she wasn't winning, it was more comfortable if I let her win, so she didn't think I was trying to be top dog.

> I go down to the basement to ask my father if he wants to play. He's sitting at his desk, a large maple desk with lots of drawers. Like his workshop, his desk drawers are well organized, with all of the office supplies in one drawer, the used batteries in another along with old radios that he has planned to fix for years, and piles of

odds and ends that might come in handy one day. A child of the Depression, my father saves all kinds of things in case they might come in handy one day.

One drawer holds a pile of old rubber bands. When he goes for walks, he picks up rubber bands on the street when he sees them. "No sense wasting them," he says.

I've been on walks with him, and he couldn't pass by a rubber band without picking it up and placing it carefully in his pocket for possible future use.

Almost everything he owns has rubber bands around it—papers, batteries, pens, cameras, even the pencil holder and the stapler—as if he's trying to hold things together in his life with all those rubber bands. Sometimes he even wears a rubber band around some of his fingers.

He's working on his graphs again.

"Mom wants to play cards. You want to join us?"

He looks longingly at the graph. I imagine he'd much rather have me listen to him some more.

"I guess so." He usually joins in reluctantly, and the games are much quieter and less enthusiastic than when my mother and I play alone.

I wonder now if my father really preferred to be by himself, but I always felt a need to include him in whatever we were doing. I thought he'd be forgotten altogether if I didn't. And I knew how awful it felt to be forgotten.

I was the peacekeeper in my family. I tried to give my father the attention he seemed to long for, and I tried to satisfy my mother's every whim and pay attention to her when she needed an audience or a mirror. I remember the anxious, edgy feeling of running back and forth emotionally from one to the other, trying to keep them happy, trying to keep them on an even keel, trying to keep myself safe from their anger, their rejection, their criticism. I became a dedicated codependent. My life's work was fixing other people's problems and offering unlimited unconditional understanding—all in the interest of keeping myself safe from the monsters that I thought lived inside other people, in the hopes that if I worked at it hard enough and kept them at bay long enough, the monsters would go live somewhere else. Until I was in my thirties and started therapy, I didn't even quite realize that I was a separate person from my parents. I didn't know I had needs until I was in my forties. I didn't start taking care of myself until my fifties, when my parents were gone.

In our family, a daughter's duty was to be there for her parents, to find a way to cope with whatever they threw at her.

My father gave my mother forty dollars a week for groceries for the four of us, and anything she could save out of that became her own spending money. My mother was always hunting through the coupon section of the newspaper, and she was very pleased with herself when she could tell us at the dinner table how little she had spent to fix us a healthy meal.

"The potatoes were only 27 cents a pound, and I got the meat on sale," she would say. "Of course, we already had the pickles, and the spinach is from our garden. So that brings the cost of our meal to about 35 cents each." My father would look pleased, and Michael and I would wonder why we were only worth 35 cents a meal.

As an adult, I understand the importance of thrift and saving money. And I know that I was lucky to have had enough. But back then, when my mother spelled out how cheaply we were eating, I thought that money was way more important than anything else in life.

My father kept a very tight rein on money, and it felt like there was never enough of anything—money, love, attention, fun. Money was the only thing in the household he could control, and he did so with a vengeance. My mother became a very savvy shopper in an effort to save as much for herself as possible out of the grocery money. I didn't blame her. Because she had grown up wearing hand-me-downs, clothes were her passion, and that's where most of the leftover money went. She once said that my father told her she could always ask him for money, but she didn't like to. The few times I had asked him for my allowance made me nauseous enough that I immediately understood why she didn't. He would look at me in consternation, his eyes narrowed, his jaw tightening and his shoulders stiffening, as if I didn't even deserve what I already had, and I could almost feel his hand clenching the coins in his pocket as if he was trying to determine whether I was worth anything at all. I understood deep inside myself that money was way more important than I was. Sometimes it seemed as if money was the true God in our family.

In spite of the fact that my father loved to talk about his investments and kept track of every penny my parents spent, he neglected to teach me anything about basic financial fitness other than "Save your money and invest it wisely." My parents needed someone to carry all the feelings of lack they had left over from growing up during the Depression—but had denied—and I was elected to be the Poor Little Match Girl.

The only way I got attention from my father, besides being there for him when he needed someone, was to be poor. When I was an adult, the only time he really expressed concern for me was when I went into debt or needed money. Though he didn't always send money, still, he would give me his full attention, his sympathy, his compassion—perhaps because he understood what it was like to live in deprivation, or perhaps to convey the message that he was pleased I wasn't outdoing him financially. I discovered years later in therapy that I had unconsciously kept myself poor so I could get his attention. The only trouble was, having grown up feeling like life was all about deprivation, I didn't realize that viewpoint was simply one perspective. I thought it was a full-fledged aspect of my identity.

When I lived in New York City in my twenties and thirties, I didn't have a piano, and my father occasionally sent me a little money so I could rent a studio and keep up my piano skills. More often, he would tell me he was going to send something, and then not get around to it. Or sometimes weeks would pass before the check he had promised for the piano studio would show up.

For many years when I visited, my mother would give me a little cardboard "Blessing Box" from the church in which she had collected her extra change over the previous months. Printed on the side in beautiful script was the Bible verse, "Blessed are the poor, for they shall inherit the Kingdom of Heaven." She always made a big deal about giving me that box with the few dollars of change in it.

I knew that on some level she truly wanted to help me out financially, and that she didn't have much to give, but since the Blessing Boxes were meant for the poor, the underlying message was that I was the poor one in the family. She was telling me who I was in her eyes without ever speaking a word, reminding me to step back into the box of daughter. It was a clear and disheartening message.

The sense of deprivation was pervasive throughout my childhood. My father's family had been very poor during the Depression, and sometimes, when a church had no money, my grandfather was paid for his ministerial services with furniture or dishware, so my parents had some very lovely things. But they didn't use them. They were solidly focused on thrift, on saving the beautiful things for some undefined distant day. I never knew why.

One of the major confusions of my childhood was that we had all this beautiful furniture and gorgeous dishware, but running alongside them like an image in a mirror was a deep and unwavering sense of deprivation. It was like living in two worlds at once, and I never knew which was the right one.

I wonder sometimes if my parents believed that God wanted us to deprive ourselves. Perhaps we were holier that way, somehow.

We had a wonderful collection of classical and opera records which nobody ever played. Some of them were fancy sets, and I used to look at the covers, with their beautiful colors and pictures of happy people dancing and having a good time, and wonder why we couldn't have a life like that. Everything seemed so drab and colorless in our house, except when the monsters came out.

And there were Grandma Mayfield's dishes—always referred to as "Grandma Mayfield's dishes"—a lovely set of creamware dinner plates and cups and saucers that she had painted with gold rims and a fancy "M" on them for Mayfield. We used them only occasionally, and they were treated with great respect. I wondered why dinners with those dishes always seemed to feel kind of sad and somber more than fancy.

Years later, my father told me that when Grandma Mayfield was grieving for a daughter she'd lost to diphtheria at the age of four, she was given those plates to paint so she would have something to do while she was mourning. The plates never looked the same to me after that, and I realized that maybe some of my father's reticence was the result of his mother's difficulty in bonding with a second child when she had already lost one.

As my father aged, he became more and more quiet. He often fell asleep when company came, because he wasn't involved in the conversation. The only thing that interested him was keeping track of his investments and recording all expenditures down to the penny. It seemed like the only thing he felt comfortable relating to was money. My mother wanted more and more attention as she aged, and when company came, after introductory pleasantries, she took over the conversation, and my father just took a nap. My mother stopped trying to include him, and the weight of trying to alleviate his loneliness fell even more heavily on my shoulders.

In many ways, I imagine my father was as dissatisfied with life as my mother was. He just kept quiet about it. Nothing could make either of them happy, and I wonder if they were afraid that if they were happy about something, something else would go terribly wrong.

I loved my father deeply. We were very similar in temperament, in our enjoyment of solitude, in our appreciation of peace and quiet. We were both earth signs. He was a hard worker, a wonderful provider, and a prime example of "Do unto others as you would have them do unto you." He lived his beliefs, and he had a good heart. The focus of his life was making others happy, and except for his rage at my brother for not doing what my father thought he should do, my father didn't allow his own frustrations and irritations to get in the way.

When my parents were in their seventies, they moved into a cottage in an assisted living complex, and my father lost his workshop. He kept his tools in the carport, but it wasn't the same. He had lost his sense of self. He tried to find himself again with his computer—he had one of the original Tandy computers in the 1980s—but it couldn't take the place of his workshop. Without the ability to make things, he was lost, and he stayed lost for the rest of his life. He began showing signs of dementia shortly after moving to the cottage, and it grew steadily worse throughout the remaining fifteen years of his life.

# Chapter 5:  The Birthday Party

When I was seven years old, my mother had a birthday party for me. That year, my birthday was the day before Easter, and my mother created a special birthday cake to commemorate both occasions at once.

It's the morning of the party. I'm so excited about having my friends over for a party that I feel like rubber balls are bouncing in my feet. My mother shows me the cake right before the party.

We stand next to each other in the tiny, clean kitchen with small windows, pink tile, and pink metal cabinets. I push up on my tiptoes, and I can barely see the cake over the edge of the counter. It's bright green, and there are some jellybeans and other things on it. The green frosting on the cake looks strange on the silver foil in the pink kitchen. I'm not sure what to make of it.

My mother is smiling as she makes swirls in the frosting with the spatula. "What do you think?" she asks.

I don't know what to say. I'm not sure whether it's real food, or just a pretty decoration.

"What is it?" I ask.

"It's a bunny cake."

"What's a bunny cake?"

Her voice begins to rise. "I made it for the party, and for Easter."

I look up at her, wondering why she doesn't answer my question.

She's looking at the cake with pride, as if it's the most beautiful thing she's ever seen. I want her to look at me the way she looks at the cake. I want her to love me the way I love her.

"Why is it green?"

Sending a warning sigh of exasperation in my direction, she says, "Because it is."

The rubber balls in my feet bounce faster as a

little fear creeps in. But I want her to look at me, not the cake, so I keep asking. "Are we going to eat it?"

She slams the spatula down on the counter, and turns an irritated glare on me. It's The Look. I feel like someone is grabbing the back of my neck, and my shoulders hunch.

"Yes!" The doorbell rings.

I have to stop asking questions now, because my friends are here. I don't want my mother to be mean to me in front of my friends.

My mother looks back at the cake, touches the edge of it gently, and lovingly adjusts one of the bunny's eyes. She pats my shoulder offhandedly as she goes to answer the door—just a quick touch, but enough to give me hope.

After my friends arrive, we gather around the table for our cake and ice cream, saving the highlight of the party—opening presents—for last. My mother brings the cake out to the table, and sets it down with a flourish.

"There!" she says, as if she's brought the moon and stars and set them down for all of us to see. "Now each of you can get up on the chair here and look at the cake." Suddenly it feels like it's my mother's party, not mine.

She helps each of us stand up on the chair, one at a time, to look at the bunny cake. Now I can see the whole cake, and my mother's words finally make sense. The cake is shaped like a bunny's head, with bunny ears, whiskers, and jellybean eyes. But it's so green, almost neon. I've never seen anything like it.

"It's a bunny," I say. My mother grabs me down off the chair, and pulls Debbie over to get up on the chair next.

My friends seem as surprised as I am to discover that someone can make a bunny out of a cake, and they don't know exactly what to make of it. We're used to plain round or square cakes, and sometimes new things are a little scary, so no one knows exactly what to say. We're still trying to cope with the question of whether or not it's okay to bite into a chocolate Easter bunny. It makes me feel a little mean to bite a bunny's head off.

Most of my friends say something like, "Oh, it's a bunny," or "Are we going to eat it?" My mother's face is twisting into a scowl, but my friends are in high spirits, looking forward to games and fun.

The smell of just-baked birthday cake wafts through the room as everyone sings Happy Birthday, and I feel waves of excitement whooshing around the table. I'm excited to get to the presents, because my parents usually give me things like socks and watches for my birthday, and I'm hoping my friends have brought dolls and games and other fun birthday toys.

The candles are lit, and I'm trying to think of a wish. There are so many things to wish for. I close my eyes, and wish with all my heart that I can finally make my mommy happy, and then I blow and blow at the candles until every last one is out. Everyone claps, except my mother, who is already taking the candles out of the cake one by one.

"Quiet, now. Quiet, everyone," my mother orders, like a queen with her servants. "I'm going to cut the cake." The clapping and murmuring stops, and the smoky smell from the candles drifts up, making us all anticipate the first taste of cake and ice cream.

My friends watch as my mother takes a knife to the bunny cake, her sharp elbows and stiff hands with big knuckles straining to cut the squares all exactly the same size and lift them cleanly off of the tray onto our plates. She works quickly and decisively, her white acrylic sweater sleeves pushed up tight on her muscular forearms, her upper body zinging back and forth from the cake to the plates, her white apron perfectly clean and starched. Her glasses slide down her pointy nose, and she gets a little frosting on them when she pushes them back up. Two of the girls giggle, but when my mother looks up at them, with the big knife held tightly in her hand, they stop.

One of my friends, Maureen, is biting her lip, as if she's wondering whether cutting the bunny cake up is hurting it. I'm not sure either, but I hope it doesn't. My mother quickly passes the paper plates of cake around the table. When she places a plate in front of me, she puts it down so fast that the cake lurches onto its side, almost falling off the plate.

"Oh, no!" my mother says, frowning at me as if it's my fault. "Now I have to wipe the crumbs off the table!" She drops the knife on the cake, and it cuts off one of the bunny ears and hits the remaining jellybean bunny eye, which bounces over to land on a whisker. We all stare at the cake while she hurries into the kitchen. My face gets hot, and the dark hand of guilt squeezes my heart. I want to crawl under the table and disappear.

My mother hurries back with a towel, and quickly wipes the crumbs off the table as I hold my plate up. I feel her annoyance in my nerves, burning just under the surface of my skin, and I put the plate down and rub my arms, but it won't go away. It's really uncomfortable. The party has gone all wrong, my mother is upset, and I have to fix things somehow.

"Thank you for the cake, Mommy. It's really pretty." I give her the biggest smile I can muster, but she doesn't say anything. I wait for her to look at me, but she doesn't, so I pick up my fork and look at my cake.

I'm a little afraid to eat the cake, because the frosting is so green. It's not a normal food color. I carefully put the first piece in my mouth, and discover that it's a luscious chocolate cake, the frosting smooth and creamy. The sweet frosting is my favorite part. I love rolling it around on my tongue as it melts, feeling the smooth sweetness glide all the way down to my toes. My friends are murmuring about how good it is, how green it is, how much they like birthday parties, and my mother seems to relax a little as the compliments leap her way. But I still have to watch her every minute, just in case.

After we finish our party feast, my mother grabs the cake tray and hurries into the kitchen. Pots and pans are banging in there, and my friends all look toward the kitchen. Then one of the cabinet doors slams in the silence, and my mother appears in the doorway, holding a plastic bag with something in it, and a stack of newspapers. I wad my napkin up in my hand and hold it tightly. She says, "Wipe your faces. We're going to play a game." Excitement ripples through the group. Maureen starts to bounce in her chair, but she stops when my mother glares at her.

Shoving the newspapers under one arm, my mother comes to the table and starts stacking the paper plates. We all rush to help, passing silverware along until it's all in a pile by the stack of plates, careful not to get crumbs on the table.

Herding us all down the hallway and into my parents' bedroom, my mother leaves the plastic bag and the newspapers in the hall, and comes into the bedroom to gather us into a circle. My mother seems even taller than she usually does, towering over us like the giant from Jack and the Beanstalk. Her eyes are very bright, and her smile looks too big. My nerves are still burning, and fear starts to creep up on me like an army of furry black spiders. I think my friends are feeling that something is wrong, because no one is saying a word.

"Quiet, everyone, quiet!" my mother says, too loudly.

Maureen is next to my mother. She jumps at the sound of my mother's voice and backs up two steps. Scowling, my mother grabs Maureen's arm, drags her back into the circle, and holds her there with both hands. Maureen doesn't struggle, but her body is as far away from her arm as she can get it. I know exactly what she feels like.

"This game is called Egg-Step," my mother explains in her most polite voice, still scowling, still holding on to Maureen. "Each of you will put on a blindfold, like you do in Pin the Tail on the Donkey, but instead of pinning the tail on, you'll walk one at a time through the hallway to the living room." She smiles again, like she knows a big secret. "I'm going to put down some newspapers on the carpet, and then some raw eggs. Those are the booby traps, and you have to be careful when you walk so you don't step on any of the eggs." Her smile is even stretchier now, so all of her teeth are showing, like the Big Bad Wolf in Little Red Riding Hood. Then she looks right at me, and I feel her eyes boring into me like tiny drills. "Raw eggs would make a mess of the carpet," she says sharply. "And then I'd have to get it cleaned."

All of a sudden I know this isn't a real party game, it's something my mother made up. The clamminess comes over me quickly. My hands starting shaking, and my stomach does a loop-de-loop, because I'm afraid this will be one of those things that's supposed to be fun, but somehow turns into something horrible that makes me dry up inside.

"Anyone who can make it through the hall without stepping on an egg will win a prize. Now you girls wait here while I set up the game." My mother strides out of the room a little crookedly, like she's being pulled on a string. She slams the door behind her.

In the sudden silence, I look around at my friends to see what they're thinking. My friend Rebecca looks like a toy soldier in her ruffled dress because her arms are stiff by her sides, and she's bent over a little as if she has the same feeling in her stomach that I do. Is she thinking my mother must be really strange? Or does her mother do things like this, too? My friend Angie's eyes look as big as light bulbs.

It isn't just the carpet I have to worry about. I'm wearing my new shoes. Most kids in my neighborhood have one special pair of good shoes that they wear only to Sunday school and birthday parties, and we get in really big trouble if we mess up our special shoes. I know I'll get in trouble if I step on even one egg, and I figure the other kids will, too. If that happens, they won't be my friends any more. And my mother might go and get my dad's belt if we step on the eggs. But we have to go along with what my mother says, because we're kids.

We sit quietly in the bedroom while my mother sets up the game in the hallway. The ticking of the clock seems to get louder and louder. The jars and bottles on my mother's vanity gleam in silent reproach. Nobody says anything. Nobody looks at anybody else. The party mood is gone, and anxiety is lurching back and forth between the walls like guitar strings gone wild.

My mother comes back in the room, carefully shutting the door behind her so we can't see the booby traps. She's holding something behind her back, and wearing a big, happy smile. "Kathy gets to go first because she's the birthday girl," she says in a singsong voice as she puts her arm around me and squeezes my shoulders. She waves a blindfold in front of my face, and then ties it around my head. It's too tight, but I'm afraid to say anything because she already seems angry. My eyes feel squished, my head hurts from the blindfold, and everything is black. I can't see even a crack of light under the blindfold.

I hear my mother open the door to the hall, and then she pushes me to the doorway. I can hear the newspaper crackle under the toes of my shoes, my mother giggling. My legs don't want to go—they want to run somewhere far away where things like this don't happen. But I can't see, and there's nowhere to run, and I can't say out loud that I don't want to go.

"You can't run away with a blindfold on," my mother whispers behind me. How did she know what I was thinking? My hands go cold, and I close them into fists, but it doesn't make me feel any better.

I step forward, and something cracks. My cake and ice cream want to come back up, so I swallow hard and clamp my lips. My hands are sweaty, but I don't want to wipe them on my dress, because I know my mother is watching.

I can almost feel the sticky, gooey egg running over my new shoes, and I try to be really careful with each step. I take more steps, hearing only the crackling of the newspaper. Maybe it will be okay. But then I hear another crack, and my mother's hand suddenly grabs mine and pulls me another two steps. She yanks the blindfold off, and I gasp because some of my hair, caught in the knot, gets ripped out when she yanks. The light is too bright, and I take a step backwards in case she's going to swat me for stepping on some eggs. But she's already walking back down the hall to get the next party guest.

I swallow the lump in my throat, and look down at the carpet to see how big a mess I've made. But something is odd. I look really hard, but I don't see any eggs. All I see are soda crackers, scattered along the length of the hallway. There are crushed crackers in the two places I thought I had stepped on eggs. I start to breathe faster. I look down at my shoes. They look perfectly fine. I feel tears welling up, but I won't let myself cry. Sometimes my mother gets even meaner when I cry, when she says, "Stop that now, or I'll really give you something to cry about!"

My mother reappears in the doorway with my friend Debbie, who has the blindfold on. She looks at me as I sniffle, and her mouth gets tighter. I swallow again, gulp in some air, and push my lips into a smile to show her I'm not crying.

It looks to me like Debbie doesn't want to go through the hall either, but she doesn't say anything. We don't talk back to adults. My mother tiptoes in a zigzag along the hall to the other end like a happy leprechaun, stepping around all the crackers as she goes, and crouches down like a lion ready to spring.

"C'mon, Diana." She always gets my friends' names wrong. "Don't step on any booby traps." She looks at me and laughs, but it doesn't sound real, more like a cartoon on TV. Debbie waves her hands around, looking for something to hold on to, and then she pats the newspaper with her toe, checking for eggs. She takes a few steps before she crunches a cracker, then she stops.

"Just a little further," my mother encourages, and Debbie starts creeping along the hallway again. My mother grabs some crackers from the box next to her and breaks them up with her fingers so it sounds like an egg is cracking every time Debbie puts her foot down. Debbie starts to shake, and her mouth scrunches up like she's going to cry. By the time she reaches the end of the hallway, she has her arms across her stomach.

My mother jerks the blindfold off, and Debbie yelps, "I have to go to the bathroom." She disappears around the corner. She doesn't even look at the carpet. My mother tiptoes down the hall again to fetch the next victim.

The cake and ice cream have turned into a sour lump in my stomach. I can't believe I'm seeing this. That's why she had me go first. I look at my mother kneeling at the end of the hallway, watching like a hawk as my friends walk carefully one by one through the hall with their blindfolds on and their bodies tensed, wincing at every little crack. She breaks crackers up with her fingers on almost every step. Her face is twisted sideways, with her lips pulled up and her teeth showing, as if she's smiling and growling all at the same time. Her eyes are shooting darts down the hall as she angrily breaks the crackers up, but she's smiling, too, with her eyebrows up, as if she's enjoying herself.

I feel like my skin is being peeled off, and I back up to the very end of the hallway. I want to be as far away as I can in case my mother with the monsters inside of her turns in my direction.

Rebecca is the last to go through. My mother pulls the blindfold off of Rebecca's head, and turns around, smiling, to see the rest of us huddled like rabbits at the end of the hall. She stares at us for a moment, her smile pasted in place, and we draw a little closer together. Rebecca hurries over to join us. My mother's grin fades to a small, sad smile, and her eyes go soft, like she might cry. I feel sorry for her, because it doesn't seem like she got whatever she wanted after all. Her shoulders droop as she turns slowly back to the hallway and says, "Go ahead, open the presents."

My friends and I turn as one, and move as fast as we can without running into the living room, where the presents wait on the coffee table in a pretty pile. We crowd into a tight circle, and I open the presents in a rush so the party will be over and my friends can get out of there and go home.

I see the relief on each of my friends' faces when their mothers come, and they realize they can leave. They can go home where it's safe.

I think my mother hates me, but I don't know what I did to make her feel that way.

After that, each time I asked one of my friends to come to my house to play, she would say she was playing with someone else, or her mother wouldn't let her, or she had to get home for dinner instead.

Most days, I tried very hard to be a Good Little Girl, especially when my mother woke up sad or mad. If she woke up sad, it made her feel better if I was sad, too. If she woke up mad, I tried to be the best Good Little Girl I could. She was always busy when I wanted something from her—she was cooking or cleaning or making an afghan or talking on the phone; or even if she was reading, she'd say, "I'm busy. Why don't you play with your dolls?"

The only time I got good attention from my mother was when I was helping her. Mondays I helped her do laundry, Tuesdays we did the dusting and vacuuming, Wednesdays we mopped the floors, and Thursdays she cleaned the kitchen while I cleaned the bathroom. On Friday nights we played cards, and had popcorn. On Saturday afternoons I helped my dad wash the car or do yard work. Sundays we went to church, and then out to eat, and then my mother would work on her crafts in the afternoon and my dad would go down to his workshop. Every week was the same, like we were a robot family. And I continued to live like a Good Little Girl robot for most of my adult life, because I didn't know any other way.

But deep down underneath the Good Little Girl, I stacked my anger and resentment layer by layer, unconsciously sculpting it into an invisible, festering pile which gathered strength with each criticism my mother aimed at me. By the time I was seven, I was so good at playing the Good Little Girl that I was blissfully, utterly unaware of the pile until many years later.

My mother excelled at keeping a nice house and providing nutritious meals. Because my father was an engineer, our life was like a well-run corporation with a long list of by-laws: dinner had to be on the table at exactly 6 p.m., everything had a place and was supposed to be in it, ashtrays were dumped and washed when they had three or four butts in them. Feet were always wiped, coats were always hung exactly so, hands were always washed before dinner. We lived by rote, by rules and regulations, which left our hearts and our hopes and our yearnings out of the equation. Any deviation from the regime received a sharp comment or swift and angry retribution. But when my father was gone and my brother was at school, my mother ruled the house with her whims and desires, dragging me along emotionally like a cat playing with a mouse.

By the time I grew into my teens, I was a robot. I had forgotten how to think. I just went along with whatever anyone else wanted to do. If someone asked me what I liked or what I wanted to do, I said, "I don't know." If I didn't want to do something, I did it anyway, because I didn't know how to say no and make it stick. I had no boundaries at all. I didn't know how to make decisions; I didn't even know I had choices. The world was programmed for me by my mother's whims, and I just went along with it. And I knew by then that if I wanted something, I would never get it, even if I worked at it forever.

Time after time, I hid parts of myself in the walls of my inner void, until all that was left was the polite me, and it ruled my life for many years. The real me hid at the bottom of the void, waiting for my turn.

# Chapter 6: Family Photos

Family photos were revered in our household, the only possessions that were more important than the beautiful things which were passed down from my parents' families. My father had boxes and boxes of old family photos stored with his cameras, and he often took them out to show to me.

The photos were packed carefully in tissue paper, and kept in a corner of the basement that was dry and cool. My father would invite me to sit down, and then he would gently and reverently open the box and unwrap some photos. He would name all the relatives in them that he could remember.

"This is your grandfather, who was a very well-regarded minister, and my mother when she was a little girl. That's Uncle Ellis." The faces in the photos were always stiff and unhappy, and I knew why. If their family life was anything like ours, they had their reasons. When we were done, my father would carefully pack the photos back into their tissue paper as if he were putting a baby to sleep for the night.

But the only photo I remember actually being out in view in our house was a photo of Aunt Mae and Uncle John, my father's aunt and uncle. They were an absolutely wonderful couple, and my parents loved them very much.

The only time I remember seeing my father truly happy was when he was with Uncle John, who loved jokes as much as he did. And years after Aunt Mae had passed away, my mother said, "Oh, I miss her so much! She was a wonderful lady, and she always made me feel good about myself. She was such a good soul." And she truly was.

The drive to visit Aunt Mae and Uncle John took about two hours. My mother always suggested that I take along some books and games to keep myself occupied. After we got out of the city, she would turn around to see what I was doing, which was invariably reading. She would say, "Put down your book, and pay attention to what's going on around you!" I would look out the window at the cows and barns, and the other cars, and wonder why they were more important than books, and why my mother wanted me to bring books if she didn't want me to read them.

Aunt Mae and Uncle John were always tickled pink when we came to visit, and I felt pretty pink about it myself. When we visited, it always felt like we were a real family. I got as much attention from them as my parents did; not like at home, where my mother had to have all the importance. I felt as important as everyone else to Aunt Mae and Uncle John, and it was a wonderful, warm feeling.

Their front door would be opening just about the time we pulled into the driveway next to Uncle John's Cadillac, as if they'd been watching for us through the window. By the time we opened the car doors, Aunt Mae would be down the steps and waiting at the bumper, with Uncle John a few feet behind her.

"Wellllll, look who's here!" she would say, her voice so full of pleasure and her face so bright and smiling that I wanted to wiggle like a puppy.

"It's the Mayfields!" Uncle John would boom, by this time shaking my father's hand and clapping him on the back. Aunt Mae would crouch down and kiss me on the cheek and say, "Wellll, aren't you pretty today?" They sure knew how to make guests feel welcome.

Aunt Mae and Uncle John had never had children. I never knew why, but I always felt like a treasured child when I was with them.

Aunt Mae was a true lady in every sense of the word. She wore elegant, tasteful dresses and suits in lovely, deep colors like blue and burgundy that somehow went perfectly with her reddish hair, and she always dressed her clothes with a pretty, graceful pin or bracelet which matched or harmonized with understated but unusually designed earrings. Her wing-tip glasses had tiny jewels in the corners. When we went out to eat, she opened a beautiful flowered compact right after dinner, and powdered her nose and reapplied her lipstick at the table. She spoke and moved in a very gentle, refined way, and had a ready, genuine smile. She was a gracious and welcoming hostess, and if you needed anything—anything at all—she was happy to provide it as best she could. She never had a bad word to say about anyone, though my mother once told me that Aunt Mae had suggested that my father was a tightwad. But I could never be sure if my mother was telling the truth or not.

Aunt Mae played the organ for their church in Louisiana, Missouri, and she loved to hear me play the old white piano in their Victorian house. I was fascinated with the piano stool, which had a white metal base and a beautiful rounded wooden seat which I could raise or lower by turning it one way or the other. We had a black piano bench at home, so the stool was a novelty. I liked to sit on it and spin round and round, first one way, then the other. It made me feel graceful and flowing.

Aunt Mae was always so very pleased when I played the piano. She would say, "Oh, isn't that just lovely!", and her applause and enjoyment encouraged everyone to join in. Even though she played the organ, she still loved my playing. There was no feeling of competition from her, only her encouragement and our sharing of the gift of music. There was space for both of us to play beautiful music, and I was free to let my skill and talent shine. I could see why my mother loved her so much. I certainly did.

Uncle John was quite a contrast to his lovely wife. He smoked unfiltered Lucky Strikes, and could blow a perfect smoke ring, and then blow a perfect smaller smoke ring through it. He always drove a used Cadillac in very good condition, and he lived to crack jokes. He had a warm and gravelly voice when he spoke, but when he sang "Bless This House," the walls themselves shivered with delight along with the rest of us. His head was mostly bald and shiny, comfortingly round, with nicely combed tufts of white over both ears and around the back. His glasses had dark frames. Both he and Aunt Mae were pleasingly plump, which made them very soft to snuggle up against when I was small—which I got up the courage to do a couple of times when my mother's attention was elsewhere.

Uncle John worked for an advertising agency called McLaughlin & Company, and his business cards and pens and calendars dubbed him "Honest John Mayfield." He could bark like a dog, and when we went out to a restaurant, Michael and I would beg him to bark. He'd let out a few barks, sounding like a big, mean dog, and invariably the waitress would come over and say, "I'm sorry sir, there are no dogs allowed in the restaurant," as she peered around uncertainly, looking for the beast. He was always good for a laugh, and it was never at anybody's expense.

One of Uncle John's best jokes was the time he went out to get a pizza and bring it back for the rest of us. His car pulled up in front of the house, and the unusually loud slam of the door brought us all to the front window. We watched him walk toward the house, whistling and carrying the pizza sideways under his arm like a notebook as he sauntered up the front walk and into the house. We all gasped, and Aunt Mae ran to get a towel to clean up what she was sure would be tomato sauce dripping on her rugs. But Uncle John was laughing as he opened the box. It was empty. He had asked for an extra pizza box for the joke, and the real pizza was waiting in the car.

We always played cards when we visited, and it was always fun. Not like when we played at home, where you didn't play to win (unless you were my mother), you played to keep the peace.

I remember that Aunt Mae would put the kettle on in her huge Victorian kitchen to make hot water for her tea. That was the signal that we were going to play cards.

On this visit, I'm ten years old. Michael isn't living at home anymore, so it's just five of us.

We're all milling around the table in the dining room—me, Mom and Dad, Aunt Mae, and Uncle John. The preferred game is Hearts. Uncle John gets out the deck of cards, cracking jokes as he goes. The cards are bright red, and are naturally printed with "Honest John Mayfield." My father drops a couple of one-liners—he's better at telling jokes here than he is at home. He and his Uncle John enjoy each other's company immensely.

Aunt Mae puts little lace doilies on the table by four of the chairs as she says, "Oh, John!" in a lovely voice each time Uncle John finishes a joke. Even my mother is laughing and enjoying herself. She helps Aunt Mae bring several glasses of soda pop from the kitchen. It's red and fizzy in the pretty frosted glasses with branches and leaves etched on them. Each doily gets its own glass.

Uncle John slaps my father on the back, laughing at one of my dad's one-liners. Happy feelings bounce around the room, and my mother appears again, smiling as she holds beautiful crystal cut-glass dishes of candy and nuts, followed by Aunt Mae, carrying her cup of tea.

My dad is still grinning, and he says, "That was pretty good with the pizza."

Uncle John snorts. "Fooled you, didn't I?"

We all sit down, and Uncle John shuffles the cards like an expert. He plays pinochle with his retired friends twice a week, and he can do card tricks, like cutting the deck with one hand.

I pick up my cards. I know how to play Hearts, but there must be some strategy that I don't know, because I usually lose. But nobody seems to notice, and I don't care, because I'm having such a wonderful time.

"Two of clubs, who's got the two?" Uncle John asks.

Aunt Mae looks at her hand, and says, "Oh," kind of distractedly, then pulls out the two and throws it to the center of the table. We play our cards in turn, and everything is silent for the first few tricks, except for the sounds of lips slurping liquid and teeth crunching nuts. We fall into the rhythm and enjoyment of a good game of cards.

Uncle John throws a heart on the next trick. "Gotcha!" he cackles. Everybody knows he's joking, no malice intended. Even the thoughts that are zinging invisibly around the room are nice ones.

I have to take the trick. Usually, when I end up getting quite a few hearts, I try to take them all so that everyone else will get all the points against them instead of me. But I never manage to.

I play the seven of spades. Uncle John throws the Queen of Spades, the bad card, down onto the table with a flourish.

"Fight over it, girls," he crows. I sneak a peek at my dad to see if being included in the "girls" bothers him, but I can't tell whether or not he's noticed. He has a very good poker face, and he wears it about 99% of the time.

My father plays the three of spades, and my mother plays the king. It looks like she has to take the trick. She's not looking very pleased. But Aunt Mae still has to play.

"Well," she says, gently and musically, as she puts an ace on top of the pile and pulls the cards to her end of the table. The tiny diamonds on the edge of her eyeglass frames twinkle in the light of the chandelier. "Would anyone like more soda pop?"

We never had to put on our actors' masks at Aunt Mae's and Uncle John's. We could be our real selves, and have fun, too. There weren't any monsters in their house.

Uncle John sent me outrageously funny birthday cards, signed by himself and "Maisie," which usually had five dollars tucked inside of them. The money wasn't as important to me as the knowledge that they always thought of me, even when I wasn't there. I always wished they could come and live with us.

All of us were very sad when they were gone. They both had enough points to get into Heaven at least twice, and they were loving and fun, too. I'm very grateful that they were part of our family. They helped me to learn what love felt like, to enjoy being part of a family.

Aunt Mae and Uncle John were like the grandparents I never had. I never knew either of my grandfathers—my parents were in their early forties when I was born, and both grandfathers were gone. My mother's mother, Grandma Metzger, was frightening. She only came to visit twice that I remember. One of the times she came, I was seven or eight.

As I open the door and start down the hall, I see Grandma Metzger at the other end, heading in my direction. Oops! Too late to run and hide. I give her my biggest, prettiest smile, in case that will cheer her up.

It doesn't work. Her face is all dark and pinched together, and her body is scrunched into itself like everything hurts. As she passes me, she raps her knuckles on top of my skull three times. Ouch! It sounds like she's knocking on hollow wood, but inside my head, and I get a headache right off. It doesn't help to duck—she's fast for a 76-year-old woman.

She does that whenever she passes me, or while we're standing around the table waiting for my mother to finish bringing dinner out. Grandma Metzger doesn't talk much; she just hits my head.

The first time Grandma Metzger hit me, I waited until she'd gone to bed, and then I went to find my mother.

"She bangs her knuckles on top of my head!" I told her. "It really hurts!"

One of my mother's shoulders shrugged up by her ear, and she said, "That's just her way of showing her love."

I wonder if Grandma Metzger loved my mother the same way when she was small.

Once or twice in my childhood, my mother showed me she loved me by grasping my hand, squeezing and shaking it a little, and screwing her face up into an expression that told me I was doing okay. Her gesture didn't really feel like love, but I knew that was what she meant.

We drove to Indiana every year to visit Grandma Metzger and my mother's two older sisters, Aunt Clara and Aunt Myrna. Grandma Metzger lived in a small house in a small town, with small rooms and a small backyard. We always started out with a sense of excitement: we're going on a trip! I liked sleeping in the car while my father drove. My parents had a colorful corduroy comforter and pillows in the back of the station wagon, so my brother and I could stretch out and snooze on the long drive.

We'd straggle out of the car at my grandmother's house, and approach the front door. Before we could knock, the door would fly open, and my grandmother would appear. Her face would be contorted, and she'd be wringing her hands. The first time I saw this, I wondered what tragedy had befallen her.

"Hi, Mom," my mother would offer. She would grasp her mother in an awkward hug, and a few sobs would escape my grandmother.

"It's so good to see you!" Grandma Metzger would gush, her body bowed and shaking. Then her face would contort again, and she would cry, "What am I going to do when you leave?" My mother's shoulders would sag, and we would all droop empathically.

Then we filed into the house, and it was like walking into a cloud of heavy dark cotton air. There was always a funny smell that I couldn't define, like really old misery. The fog of sadness seemed to infiltrate the very air in her home, to mysteriously crawl out of nowhere and cover all of us with a fine mist of unhappiness. The house exuded a miasma of staleness and unused life, as if the things that lived there were no longer seen or cared for, and hadn't been for a long, long time. The doilies sat stiff and sad under their fragile little china pitchers, and all the wood furniture felt dead. It was hard to move in that house, as if misery were taking up so much space that there were only little pockets where life was allowed.

My grandmother's house helped me to imagine my mother's childhood, and in doing so, to give her more attention and understanding than I might have otherwise. I didn't like it there. It felt like a house of despair, the kind you see in a scary movie before the monster comes.

I liked visiting my Aunt Clara's house, though. There was a small organ in the living room, which she played with such gentle passion I thought she was an angel on earth. She and Uncle Hal had a nice cottage near the woods, with pet bunnies outside, and cats, of course, and an extra little cottage that we stayed in overnight. It had a good smell, comforting like a mix of cookies and pine trees and the bear I slept with at night when I was small.

There was a pool table in the living room of our cottage, and though I didn't know how to play, I loved to watch the shiny, brightly colored balls roll across the table and into the pockets, creating order out of chaos and promising fun.

My uncle has a workshop in another little building, with all kinds of machinery and tools and scraps of wood and metal. He's helping me make a spinning top out of a round bar of metal.

"It's called a lathe. You reach up here to set the size of the cut you want." He stands behind me and shows me how to adjust it, placing his wiry hands over mine. I notice the thin gray hairs on his arms. I want to lean back into him, but I'm afraid to. "Then you place the bar right here, right next to the blade. Hold it on both ends, that's right, keep your hands away from the blade." I soak up his attention. He gives me goggles to protect my eyes, and I think he really cares about me. I want to make the very best top I can.

"Now as you go, you move the top in and out to shape it, see?" He guides my hands, and together we form a lovely, shining metal top, and when I try it on the floor, it spins for a long time.

"Good job!" he says. I want to make more things; mostly I just want him to keep paying attention to me, but we have to go back over to the cottage for dinner.

In contrast to my uncle's wiriness, my aunt was pleasingly plump, with black hair folded gently into a loose bun, warm eyes, and large, strong hands. She was a Christian Science Practitioner, and she had a sweet little office on the side of the house, decorated in red gingham and sporting a real cuckoo clock, where she counseled people. She was also a very good amateur painter, and several of her oil paintings hung there in the cottage.

My aunt had loads of dolls with china heads. Some had painted black hair, as black as my aunt's hair was, and some had real hair—shining blond or brown curls tied with ribbons. The dolls lived on high shelves that went all the way around the living room and dining room. There must have been at least a hundred of them.

Once in awhile, she let me play with one. She would gently sit me down in one of the comfy over-stuffed chairs, pick a doll from the high shelf, and bring it to me. Most of them were quite large and took up my whole lap. She placed the doll in my arms with great care, smiling tenderly at me, and once I remember she petted the doll's hair, then petted my hair for a moment. The doll was so beautiful, with light pink brushed across its china cheeks, exquisite black painted eyes and eyebrows, and perfectly formed pink lips. She was dressed in a frilly, lacy blue satin dress, and had little blue cloth shoes on its feet. I was so frightened of breaking the doll that all I could do was sit there and hold her on my lap, but it was a very lovely feeling.

The dolls looked so real, and they were so much more beautiful than my own plastic dolls. I wished I could play with them all the time, and I wanted to stay with my aunt and uncle instead of going home, but I could never say that out loud. With her gentle, gracious manner, and a special smile that seemed like she smiled it just for me, Aunt Clara always made me feel as if she wished I were her daughter. She had two boys of her own, who were grown by the time I remember visiting, but I wondered if she always wanted a girl.

My other aunt, the oldest sister of the three, was my brother's favorite, possibly because she drank beer and was more outspoken that Aunt Clara. Aunt Myrna was a pediatric nurse who also played the organ, and she had a miniature china cat collection. I had a cat collection too, and on one visit, when I was in my twenties, she gave me several of her china cats.

Aunt Myrna's cat collection is artfully displayed in a lovely dark wooden shadow box in the dining room, and I'm admiring it after dinner as she clears the dishes from the table.

"These are really beautiful," I say, thinking of my own cat collection packed in a box in the closet at home.

She comes over to stand next to me. Her body is sharp, like my mother's, but I don't feel the air pushing in on me with her like I do with my mother.

"I've collected them all my life," she says. "I always loved cats."

"Me, too," I say. We stand for a moment, enjoying our mutual appreciation of cats.

She reaches into the shadow box and picks out a mother Siamese cat with two kittens, and a larger shiny black and white cat.

"Here," she says awkwardly, holding them out to me. "Why don't you take these with you?"

I look at the blank spaces in the shadow box on the wall, and I say, "I can't take part of your collection." It doesn't seem right that there will be blank spaces where my aunt's cats had been if I accept her gift.

"I'm not going to need them," she says simply. She takes my hand and places the cats in it.

"Thank you," I say, wanting to say more, but not sure what it is I want to tell her.

The following spring, Aunt Myrna died of cancer. She was only in the hospital for three days before she passed away. I imagine she knew what was coming, back when she gave me the cats. And I imagine that, since she was a nurse, she also knew that sometimes sick people spent the last part of their lives lying in a hospital bed in a lot of pain, fighting the terrible battle, and she didn't want her life to end that way, so she stayed at home as long as she could. I admired her a lot, but I couldn't let on, because my mother didn't approve of Aunt Myrna's beer-drinking.

My mother was born in 1916, the last of three sisters. She often noted sadly that my grandmother told her she should have been a boy, so my mother was named Jeroldine after her father, Jerold. She became a tomboy, and said herself that she was always a rebel. I imagine that her relationship with her mother was at least as difficult as mine was with her.

Her mother treated her sisters like twins, and my mother said she always felt like the odd man out. She also intimated that her sisters ganged up on her. She often said she had a close relationship with her father, but the discomfort between my mother and her sisters was very obvious to me, and was never resolved. I think my mother might have been the scapegoat in her family—the one that everybody dumped on, the one who didn't fit in with the other females.

When my mother was young, her German grandfather came to live with them in his old age, and she had a hard time with him.

"I was the one who had to cut his hair," she said. "And I had to be careful while I did it so that he couldn't get me." I didn't press her for more information, and she didn't offer it, but I can see how cutting his hair might have been pretty traumatic for her.

The same grandfather had lost a son in a drowning accident when Grandma Metzger was small, which probably accounted for some of Grandma's depression and anxiety. She used to go out on the back porch during thunderstorms and keen and wail, terrified that everything was going to be blown away. My mother grew up frightened of thunderstorms, and she told me once she was worried that she might transfer her fear to me. One of the nicest things she did for me was to set me down during storms when I was a baby, so I wouldn't feel her shaking. As an adult, I love thunderstorms, and I'm grateful to her for her foresight. But I am my grandmother's granddaughter: I can feel when the weather's changing, right in my nerves, the way I could feel my mother's moods changing.

My mother's father, Jerry, was a volunteer fireman, and she loved riding on the fire engine with the siren going, though she said the other kids were jealous. She sang his praises all my life, saying that he was always willing to help a friend in need, in fact sometimes coming home on payday with a good amount of his pay missing because someone needed food.

I wish I had met her father, just to see what he was like.

In my father's family, the only person I knew besides Aunt Mae and Uncle John was his mother, Grandma Mayfield. She was my favorite grandmother.

I loved Grandma Mayfield very much, and I could just tell she loved me, even though she wasn't very demonstrative. A tiny woman, she wore simple flowered dresses, and a blue traveling suit with veiled hat and white gloves when she came to visit.

She was the pinnacle of propriety—she had been a minister's wife, after all—quiet, polite, always offering to help without seeming to get in the way. She was a true lady 100% of the time, and a perfect model of God's love and mercy, keeping her beliefs and her opinions and any judgments she might have made all to herself. She didn't believe in interfering. What a great mother-in-law!

On one of her visits when I was around six, I went looking for her, hoping to get some attention before I went to bed.

She's in the small bathroom, the door ajar. "I'm almost done here," she says. "I'm just brushing my hair." Her hair is thick and yellow-white, and hangs almost to her waist. Most of the time, she wraps her hair up into a large bun at the back of her head. I can tell by the way she brushes it that she really loves her hair.

My eyes stray past her hair to the metal shelf above the sink, the shelf where two years ago my father left the cord to his razor plugged into the wall, and because the end of the cord looked like a little straw with two holes, I sucked on it to see what would come through. It was the biggest shock of my life! After that experience, the feelings coming from other people got much stronger.

On the shelf is a glass half-full of water, with a set of teeth in it. I stare at the teeth. My brain buzzes, and my eyes start to feel stretched open.

I've never seen anyone's teeth in a glass. I squint to make sure I'm seeing it right. I know I'm not supposed to ask questions, but I have to find out how she got them out. I'm pretty sure she won't get mad if I ask. "Are those your teeth?"

Grandma Mayfield puts her brush down, and turns to look at the teeth. Her cheeks get a little pink, like the beginnings of a pretty sunset. "Yes, those are my teeth," she says gently.

"How did you get them out?" I ask, and even before she answers, I want to know even more whether she can get them back in. I've seen her with teeth in her mouth, so she must be able to get them back in somehow.

She thinks for a moment, then shakes her head slightly. "They're dentures," she says, as if that explains everything. "Now you go on to bed, and I'll see you in the morning."

As I finish getting ready for bed, I wonder, are there other body parts that come off and go back on, like arms or legs? I have funny dreams that night.

Years later, my mother would tell me that Grandma Mayfield had gone to her, explained the situation, and said, "I just don't know what to tell her."

So the next morning when my mother woke me up, she got us all together, me and Grandma Mayfield and the teeth, and explained that sometimes people had false teeth, like I had glasses to help me see. I understood that.

It was really nice of my mother to take the time to explain right away. If she hadn't, I imagine I would have worried about my body parts coming loose for years.

Later, Grandma Mayfield let me look at the teeth while they were in her mouth, and they looked just like real teeth. Finally, some sense was made of my new discovery.

Grandma Mayfield was also very good at reading bedtime stories. Even though she was prim and proper, when I asked her for a story she would pull a chair right up next to the bed, and hold my hand and rub it gently while she read. She had a different voice for every character, and she was the only person I knew who could raise one eyebrow at a time. That was the only indication that something didn't quite sit right with her. I practiced for hours, first using my fingers, then looking in a mirror, until I could raise one eyebrow by itself. I thought that was really neat.

When Grandma Mayfield was reading to me, I always felt her love shining down on me, as if I were the most important person in the world.

When I was seven, my parents told me one day that Grandma Mayfield was sick, and they would be going to visit, while I would be staying with a friend of my mother's, a very nice lady who fed me pancakes and jam for breakfast, and taught me how to sew a hem in a skirt. I was confused in the atmosphere of her home, because she and her husband seemed to enjoy each other's company, and there didn't seem to be any monsters at all. Everything was so unfamiliar I couldn't make sense of it.

Two months later, we went to Kansas for my grandmother's funeral. It was my first, and I remember how somber it was, with everyone dressed in black or gray, and the minister up in front talking like our minister did in church, but he seemed so sad. I saw my grandmother in her coffin, but I didn't have a real understanding of death yet, and all my feelings had already gone underground, so I didn't cry. I was just numb.

I didn't grieve my favorite grandmother's death until almost 40 years later, when I began sorting through all the feelings I had hidden away in the darkest corners of my heart for so many years.

My father was born in 1915, a few short years after Grandma Mayfield had lost her daughter, Anna Lowe, to diphtheria. He got his engineering degree at Kansas State University, and became an electrical engineer. My grandfather, William Madison, threw himself into parish work, and ended up ministering to three different parishes at once when they moved to Kansas. In a photo taken in his sixties, my grandfather is emaciated, and his skin is very sallow. He died of liver cancer, and the doctor told my grandmother that he would keep the cancer a secret because at that time, in Kansas at least, it was still shameful to mention it.

The other photo I've seen of my grandfather shows him sitting in his study reading, with a glass of dark liquid at his elbow, and the fact that my father would never touch a drop of liquor, even at celebrations, makes me wonder if his father was a drinker.

I wish I had met my grandfather, just to see what he was like.

My grandfather fell ill when my father was in the Navy. The Navy granted my father leave, and the Red Cross helped him get back to Kansas so he could be with his family when his father passed away. For the rest of his life, my father gave money to the Red Cross every Christmas to express his gratitude. Shortly after being discharged from the Navy, he met and married my mother.

All of my family history was recorded in photos, and though stories were told, they were told without emotion, without any explanation of what the experiences were like. No one talked about how people coped with difficult life experiences, or how they learned or healed from them. I had to learn all of that on my own.

I imagine that my parents never healed from the emotional wounds they received early in their lives, and in my mind, that's what caused all of the drama under the surface in our family. Their own tragedies were never fully told, so they never got free of the past.

# Chapter 7: Reaching Out for Life

I enjoyed school. The structure of classes helped me to focus, and I liked the process of learning and exploring. I hoped that finally it was my turn, my chance to reach out and grab life the way my mother did. But other than being smart enough to make my teachers happy, I didn't fit in. Being the Good Little Girl pleased my teachers, but it didn't help me make friends, and I didn't know how else to be.

At six, I could play very simple pieces on the piano, and on Parents' Day, in the last week of kindergarten, I got to play a very pretty piece called "Chimes in the Mist."

> Everyone is looking at me as I play the familiar notes. The attention and interest of the audience feels good, and I like knowing I can play well. I feel special because I'm the only one in the class who gets to play, and I enjoy the applause and the bowing afterwards.
>
> But later, when I'm out on the playground during recess, one of the other girls points at me and says to her friends, "She plays the pi-A-no. She thinks she's SOOO good." My stomach sinks and I want to curl in on myself. I wish I could crawl in a hole and never come out. Suddenly I'm ashamed that I can do something well, and I instinctively know that I'll never be accepted into that group of friends. I'm too different. I can do something they can't do.
>
> This is a new feeling; usually it's my mother who can do something I can't do. But even though it seems like my accomplishment should feel good, it feels icky. The yearning to show my gifts and be appreciated for them shrivels up and hides way down in a shadowy corner of my mind.

I learned early on to hide my gifts and downplay my abilities. I shrank myself to fit the world around me.

I had no role model for learning how to make friends. The only thing I knew how to do in relationships was to let the other person have their way. I played with other kids, but I couldn't really connect with them because I didn't know how to relate to functional people. I always felt excluded from groups at school, especially during grade school, when I had braces and glasses and my nicknames were Four Eyes and Metal Mouth. All of the kids who wore glasses were laughed at. I don't know why the other kids equated vision problems with extra brainpower, but my need for vision correction and dental upgrades added to my general sense of not being good enough.

In the cafeteria, or on the playground, I would approach a group of girls, wanting to be friendly, but I didn't know what to say or how to act. I worried constantly about whether or not someone was mad at me, so I couldn't focus on and participate in the activity at hand. I had no social intelligence. I didn't know how to be a part of a group, let myself be carried along by the group's energy moving from one activity to another. I just didn't fit in, though I tried hard to make friends.

As everyone walks back to class after recess, I take a couple of skips to catch up to Joan, a thin girl with straight blond hair and smart-looking blue eyes. I'm not sure how to start a conversation, because my mother always starts them, but I desperately want a friend.

"I saw you playing hopscotch. Do you like it?" I ask Joan.

She keeps walking. "It's okay." I wait for her to say more. I'm so used to listening that it seems funny she only said two words.

My desire for connection grows, and I press on. "Do you like school?"

"Yes." She hasn't even looked at me. I start to wonder again what's wrong with me. Is it my braces? My glasses? Did I do something wrong?

We're almost at the door; I don't have much time. "Do you like to read?"

"It's okay."

I don't know what else to ask. We've reached the door, and I follow Joan into the classroom, not sure whether we're friends yet or not.

I didn't realize that I usually tried to make friends with kids who were as shy as I was. It never worked.

Because I had learned to be very vigilant at home, I usually caught on to things more quickly than some of the other kids in school. When I was in third grade, I complained to my parents that school was boring. They hunted around and found a progressive school in another neighborhood, and decided to send me there for fourth, fifth, and sixth grades. They wanted to help. Sometimes they truly did try to do what was best for me.

My new school was located in what was then called a "colored neighborhood." The school was touted as offering a very progressive education, and it absolutely lived up to its reputation. Students were tested on entering the school to determine their current level of knowledge, and then started on the program according to a graduated level. I enjoyed being able to work as fast as I could, without having to wait for other students, and I'm sure the program was helpful to students with learning disabilities as well, because they could move at their own speed, too.

There were twelve white kids in the school, and the rest of the students were black. My experience there afforded me a unique perspective for a white person: in spite of growing up in a completely WASP family and a completely WASP neighborhood, I know exactly what it feels like to be one of the minority. It's not fun. Being in the minority made me feel like I was surrounded all the time by people who were very different from me, and it was frightening. On a primordial level, I was not in my own clan. I had been plopped into a completely foreign one.

Those years gave me a level of compassion for minorities which I probably wouldn't have had otherwise. When I lived in New York many years later, I became much more accustomed to diversity.

The twelve of us were pretty much accepted by the other students, but we still stood out like neon signs. There were a few white teachers, but they were mostly quiet and deferential, inadvertently providing role models for how we should act around the other students. The African-American teachers were louder, stronger, bolder, and more confident, especially the women.

Mrs. Burnett, my fourth grade music teacher, was instrumental in showing me that I might have some worth. I had often been called a "teacher's pet" because I did well in school, but I was more than a teacher's pet with Mrs. Burnett, a tall, feisty black lady with carefully styled gray hair who always wore a nice dress and a pretty necklace. She was a wonderful teacher, and took the stage like a star when she taught, pacing back and forth like a tiger with her arms gesturing wildly as she tried to get the students interested in music. Her voice boomed out in smooth, warm contralto tones, as if she'd been singing in a church choir all her life. She was by turns colorful and bold, or tender and sweet, as if she lived with music inside of her all the time.

Mrs. Burnett loved music passionately, and she naturally appreciated the fact that I was musically inclined and could answer a lot of the questions she posed to the class. She paid lots of attention to me, and when she looked at me, I saw appreciation, understanding, encouragement, and humor in her eyes. She was the first person in my life who ever stood up for me.

When I played the piano one day in class and the other kids started snickering, she came down on them hard.

> "Now, you listen, you all!" She's got her hands on her hips, and her body is swaying back and forth, her necklace counting time like a metronome. Her eyes are flashing, like my mother's, but she's looking at the other kids, not me. Even her hair seems to be wriggling with outrage on my behalf. "Being able to play music is a true gift. It takes a lot of hard work and a lot of talent to be able to play, and maybe if some of you started *studying* instead of making fun of other people, you might be able to do something good, too!"

I don't know whether her words inspired the other kids to extend themselves into their potential, but she gave me my first experience of being supported and encouraged, of being defended instead of criticized. Mrs. Burnett made me feel important, and she made me feel good about having talent and using it. To this day, I am grateful to her for this immeasurable gift.

I wonder sometimes how my life would be different if I had never met Mrs. Burnett. My parents often told me, "Don't toot your own horn," and Mrs. Burnett was the first person to show me that there might be another side to that coin.

Most of the black kids were friendly, and fun to play with at recess. But there were occasional racial issues at the school, and sporadic violence. I had a first-hand experience with the darker side one afternoon, perhaps as a result of Mrs. Burnett's encouragement.

After lunch, I have to use the bathroom, and I ask the teacher if I can be excused. She says yes. The bathroom is empty when I push open the door, the weak sunlight trying to squeeze itself through the thick window glass with its wire reinforcement. As I'm sitting in the stall, I hear another girl come into the bathroom. Suddenly, the door in front of me starts rattling as if she's trying to open it, and her hands appear on the top of the stall door—the hands of a black girl. Her face slowly comes into view over the top of the door as she pulls herself up.

"Whaddaya doin' in there?" she says, as I close my legs and hurry to pull my skirt over my exposed parts.

I don't know what to say, and I don't know how to handle this situation. When all else fails, I pull out my politeness, because sometimes it makes people stop being mad. "I'm using the bathroom," I say, as nicely as I can.

"Hurry up! I want to come in."

We're the only ones in the bathroom, and there are three other stalls.

Something is wrong. This feels like one of the monsters at home. I didn't think there were any at school. Sweat pops out on my back and under my arms. I smell my own fear, and the tang of her anger mingles with it, creating the age-old scent of pursuer and pursued.

I try to finish my business without exposing myself again, and flush the toilet. I have a choice between staying trapped in the stall until someone else comes in the bathroom, or opening the door to the danger. I'm afraid she'll crawl under the door, and then I'll really be trapped. My only hope of escape is getting to the bathroom door, and I don't want to make her any angrier, so I choose going out.

She jumps off the door just before I open it, and slowly I step out of the stall. I feel like I'm choking, and I can't breathe. She's a little smaller than I am, but I'm afraid. I've seen some of the fights between the students here, and they aren't hesitant the way they often are in a white school. I don't know how to fight—the wrestling matches I've had with my brother only taught me how to give in quickly so I didn't get hurt.

What I really want to do is run right out the door, but my programming says I have to wash my hands after I use the bathroom, so I start towards the sink. The girl grabs my glasses off of my face and flings them onto the floor at the far end of the bathroom. I gasp because I'm afraid they're broken, and I'll get in trouble at home if they are, so I rush over, and find to my great relief that they're not.

I stand and turn to her and say, "Hey, that's not nice!" I'm hoping that I'll encourage her to apologize, and the incident will be over. But this is a different world than I'm used to. I suddenly realize that she's not going to get into the polite mode the way I expect her to.

Now she's between me and the exit, and I haven't even gotten to wash my hands yet. She steps up to me, and slaps my face hard. I don't know what to do, I don't know how to defend myself or hit back. I just take it, the way my brother takes the beatings from my dad. But I'm lucky; she's had enough. She trounces out of the bathroom, and I wash my hands and face in cold water, trying to keep the tears from overwhelming me.

I wait in the bathroom for awhile, because I don't want to meet the girl in the hallway. Finally, I open the door slowly to see if she's hiding in the hall. I don't see her, so I go back to class.

I have to tell someone what happened. I have to find a way to reorient myself in a world that's not out to hurt me, a world that's okay. I need to confirm that the outside world isn't just like home. I need to get my balance back, so I go to one of the white teachers, Mrs. Cranshaw, whose tall, angular frame is bent over the papers she's checking in the corner of the room.

"I need help," I whisper urgently.

She turns her head to look at me, leaving her hands on the work she's doing. "What's the matter?"

"One of the girls hit me in the bathroom." I'm trying to talk quietly, but my voice is getting raspy. I feel the tears rising and rising and I can hardly keep them from taking me over. "She jumped on the door, and she threw my glasses on the floor, and she hit me."

Mrs. Cranshaw peers more closely at my face, and says, "Who was it?"

I try to point without being obvious at the girl where she sits on the other side of the room. "The smaller girl with short hair in the yellow dress. I don't know her name." Mrs. Cranshaw lifts her head and looks across the room as she considers the options.

After a moment, she turns back to me and says, "Let's just let it go." She pats my shoulder briefly and smiles a small smile before she goes back to her work. My stomach sinks, and I feel even smaller. Maybe I should have told one of the black teachers instead, like Mrs. Cooper, who always says what she thinks, and sometimes gets a little pushy in a good way. But now I'm stuck. Mrs. Cranshaw won't like it if I go to another teacher after she's told me to let it go. I hold my tears in some more and push the experience to the back of my mind so I can get through the rest of the day.

When I get home, I go right to my room, grab my old bear, lie down on the bed, and burst into tears. My cheek still hurts, and I'm still frightened. What if it happens again tomorrow? I can't stop using the bathroom when I have to.

My mother comes in; she's noticed something's wrong. I'm afraid to cry in front of her, but I can't stop the tears. She says, "What happened to you?" I'm afraid to tell her what happened because somehow it will all get twisted around until it's my fault, and then I'll get into trouble, and I don't want any more pain today, I've had enough. Knowing that it's not safe for me to tell her makes me cry harder. She sits on the far end of the bed, pats my foot hesitantly, and says, "Well, you've really gotten yourself worked up, haven't you?"

After that day, the wall of fear that kept me from connecting with the world got a little bit thicker.

In many ways, my years at that school solidified the belief I'd learned at home that life was dangerous and most people were mean or uncaring. If it hadn't been for Mrs. Burnett, I might have gotten stuck in that belief forever.

Years later, when I was in my thirties, I discovered how deeply old memories can be stored in the body when I went dancing with friends at a club in New York City.

We stopped at the club's bar first to get a drink, and then headed downstairs to the dance floor. We walked in behind another group of people, and as soon as I saw the dance floor, I froze. There were probably fifty people on the darkened dance floor, and most of them were black. The memory of that day in the bathroom at school came shooting into my nerves as if I were transported right back to that place and time. I hadn't thought about the experience in years, but my body remembered perfectly. I couldn't breathe. My heart was pounding and I was clenching and unclenching my fists. I couldn't help it—the tension had to get out somehow.

I know now that when old painful experiences aren't acknowledged and released, they blurt out of the psyche in situations that have similarities to early trauma. But I didn't know that when I was at the club; I just thought I was going crazy.

I made some excuse to my friends before I scrambled into one of the chairs placed around the perimeter of the room, needing to get my back against a wall. My friends headed out onto the dance floor, and I lost sight of them. I tried to ground myself, to get hold of some part of me that wasn't that little girl from fourth grade, but I was too freaked out. I sat for awhile, drinking beer and trying to sort out my feelings, and then I realized I had to pee. I took a couple of deep breaths, and started off to search for the bathroom, my eyes bulging and my muscles twitching from the tension. I carefully pushed open the door, went in, and did my business as quickly as possible, and left, grateful that no one else came into the bathroom. Then I left the club, without even letting my friends know. The next day I left a message, telling them that I had suddenly gotten sick.

Years later, I learned in therapy that old memories can be "triggered" if there are enough similarities between a past situation and a present one, and that a person will tend to respond in the old, familiar ways to a triggering event until a new perspective is brought to bear on the situation and the person learns new options for responding.

My body has a way of reminding me about the past, even when my mind isn't focused on it. It has a memory of its own, and when I'm in a situation that's similar to a challenging situation from my childhood, it throws the memory right to the front of my brain. It's taken some practice to get my conscious mind to pay attention when that happens so I can figure out what's going on. Because a lot of my memories were repressed, for a long time the process was totally unconscious, the way it was in the club in New York, and I would have little or no idea what was happening. I would just suddenly freak out over what seemed like inconsequential issues. But when I discovered that even simple situations could trigger a past memory buried in the unconscious, I began working to make the process conscious by asking myself "What's going on?" every time I had a knee-jerk physical sensation or got popped out of reality into an unexpected but totally familiar feeling.

If we don't get to process traumatic experiences when they happen, the body stores them in our musculature. Even though many years later we may not have conscious access to them, they can be accessed and worked through to such a degree that we can regain a lot of the lost sense of self that results from a history of abuse or PTSD. It's not comfortable, but it can be done. Alice Miller's work on poisonous pedagogy and emotional trauma has been extremely helpful to me in this regard. Once the embedded memories of trauma are released, the old feelings don't pop out of nowhere when a new situation reminds me of a past experience. My perspective on events and circumstances is much more clear, and I can live without the pain-colored glasses I wore for so many years.

As an adult, I can finally feel what's going on in my body. As a child, I had to focus so much outside of myself in order to follow the rules that I had no attention left for my inner life. I had no access to a normal child's development process of learning to connect with body and emotions. Whether it's instinct or awareness, some parents know how to leave room for a child to develop a connection with self, to find his or her own rhythm. My mother didn't. I suspect it's because she never found her own rhythm, that she was forced to pick up someone else's when she was small.

For several of my childhood summers, I went to week-long summer camps at YMCA Camp Lakewood in Potosi, Missouri, about 75 miles from St. Louis. The camp was set on a beautiful lake, with rustic log cabins and a great Lodge where we ate meals and had group events like sing-alongs and contests. There were all kinds of activities: horseback riding, swimming, canoeing, crafts, archery, and of course skits, which I loved.

Canoeing was one of my favorite activities. The first time I went canoeing my counselor told me I'd have to leave my glasses on the shore, so they wouldn't get lost if I fell in the water. So I had to sit in the back of the canoe because I couldn't see where we were going. She helped us put on our life vests and get in the canoe, and then we pushed off.

I paddled for awhile on one side of the boat, then on the other, looking at the water and not paying much attention to anything else. It was nice not to have to pay attention to anything but the paddle and the water. I started enjoying myself, feeling relaxed and peaceful. The air didn't press in on me and make me feel squished there the way it did at home. I decided I liked canoeing.

The last day of camp was Family Day. Our families were invited to come for the afternoon and see the camp, and then stay for dinner before driving us home. All of a sudden there were at least three times as many people as there had been all week. After winding my way through several groups of happy families with laughing kids, I finally found my parents.

> My mother leans down to me first thing, and says, "Did you see us?"
>
> I don't understand. "What do you mean?" I ask warily.
>
> "In the canoe. We saw you the other day in the canoe." My muscles clench. I'm confused, trying to figure out how they saw me in a canoe. My mother looks puzzled. "When you were on the lake." I stare at her blankly, trying to make sense of what she's saying. Now she's looking offended, and my heart starts pounding. "We waved at you. Didn't you see us?" Her jaw moves sideways, and she squints, as if she's thinking, "Why are you so stupid?"
>
> My dad is standing with his hands in his pockets, half-smiling like he usually does, and taking in the situation blankly.
>
> Now I'm really confused. I think to myself, I was in the canoe on Wednesday, and this is Friday. I thought they were home in St. Louis all week. My brain starts to feel like a small, furry animal trapped in a cage.
>
> "You were here?" I ask. It's all I can think of to say. I want to know what's going on, I want to understand, because when I can't, it feels like I'm crazy, or stupid, or both.

Now my mother sounds irritated, and her mouth is tight. I've managed to annoy her without even trying. And now I feel stupid, as if anyone else would have understood right off the bat.

"We rented a cabin down the road a mile or two, and we saw you canoeing the other day," she says. "Why didn't you wave?"

I feel like I'm in a blender.

"I didn't have my glasses on," I plead. "I didn't see you." I think back over the week as fast as I can, and wonder if I've done anything my parents might have seen that would get me in trouble when we get home. "I'm sorry," I say, though I don't know what I'm sorry for.

"Well," my mother huffs. "Let's go see your cabin."

The next year I went, I couldn't have fun at camp because I couldn't be sure they weren't out there, watching. I just never knew what my parents were going to do.

The letters I sent home from camp were filled with protestations of love and sad descriptions of how much I missed my parents. I was afraid they would forget me and leave me at camp forever if I didn't make sure they knew I loved them. Even as a child, on some subconscious level I knew there was something missing in my relationships with my parents, and I had no real sense that I was important to them.

The third year I went to camp, I brought my friend Bernadette along. She was cool because she could blow a bubble inside a bubble when she was chewing bubble gum. One of the bubbles-in-a-bubble was as big as her head, and I took a photo of her. In the photo, she was wearing a red YMCA Camp Lakewood nightshirt, and the only thing you could see above the nightshirt was a huge pink bubble with bits of blond hair around the edges.

One of the huge bubbles popped once when somebody poked their finger in it, and the counselors had to use ice cubes to get the gum out of her hair.

Bernadette knew how to make friends, and how to have fun. She cracked a lot of jokes, and put on funny expressions, and I got a lot of attention that year because I was her friend. That was actually the first year at camp I felt like I was part of the group of girls in our cabin. We had great counselors, Johanna and Debbie, and I finally started learning how to have fun. It was about time. I was eleven that year.

The next year, my parents signed me up for a bicycle camp, and either they didn't know it was a bicycle camp or they had forgotten about it, because when we got to camp on the first day, the counselor who greeted us said, "Where's your bicycle?" My parents drove home, and my father turned around and drove back 75 miles to the camp with my bicycle that afternoon. It was a wonderful thing for him to do, and it was one of the few times I felt important and loved.

If my parents hadn't done nice things for me, like send me to camp and find a better school for me and drive all that way to bring my bicycle, their neediness and criticism and retaliation would have been less confusing. Here were these wonderful people, doing all these wonderful things for the church and the community, and occasionally for me, people that a lot of other people thought very highly of, people that obviously cared, putting me down and making me feel small and worthless. I'm sure I would have been able to get out of the box I lived in much more easily if it was all bad, but it wasn't. The fact that they did so many good deeds made me feel even more like a loser.

That's why it's taken so many years to sort through my feelings, my understanding of my parents and my relationship with them. I couldn't just say, "They were bad people," because that wasn't the whole story. The Good Little Girl had believed the world to be cast in shades of black and white—this is good, that's bad, based on what I'd learned from my parents—and in adulthood I had to learn how to differentiate innumerable shades of gray.

In my opinion, many people are afraid of looking at all the shades of gray, because when they do, they have to make choices based on their own soul-searching instead of just following what everyone else is doing.

Our family was not only dysfunctional, it was extremely insular. There was always a huge gulf between "we" and "they," the rest of the world. A lot of the difficulty I had relating to others came about because there was such a sense of "apartness" in my family mixed in with the enmeshment that I didn't know how to be "with" others, didn't know how to be on the same page with other kids, except when I was play-acting, pretending to be someone else.

My mother kept some of her old dresses and my grandmothers' old clothes in a box in the Utility Room, and I liked to play "dress-up" with them, to act out different characters. It was another chance to pretend I was someone else, to escape the reality of living in my family. Occasionally I invited one of the neighborhood kids to come over and play dress-up.

Priscilla and I are pawing through the big box of clothing. I pull out an old pink silk dressing gown with white lace.

"Oh, I'm going to wear this!" I say. "It's like a princess dress." I slide the silky softness over my shoulders, tie the belt. The gown only drags on the floor a little bit. I feel really big and special and beautiful wearing it.

Then I reach in and find one of my grandmother's dresses, a silky dark blue polyester with tiny pink and white flowers.

"Oh, that's pretty," Priscilla says. She's skinny and long-boned, with lanky brown hair and a tired look that never goes away. She has seven brothers and sisters, and I wonder what it would be like to live with so many other kids.

"Why don't you wear this?" I say. "You can play the mom."

"I don't want to play the mom," Priscilla says. "I want to play the dancer."

"But there isn't a dancer in the story," I say, even though I haven't made the story up yet. I want to be the center of attention for once. I want to be the princess, and have everyone else do what I want, like my mother gets to do.

"But I want to be the dancer," she insists.

"Okay, why don't you be the dancer, and you come to the castle to dance for the princess?"

"I don't want to go to the castle," she says. "I want to dance in Arabia, like in Arabian Nights."

I'm frustrated. I feel like I'm not going to get my turn again. I don't know how to take control, and if I just give in, I'll feel like I'm with my mother all over again.

"Okay," I say. "I'll be a princess in Arabia."

And real life went away again for a little while.

I had a recurring dream when I was a child that my brother and I were playing outside in the yard when a huge robot, about the size of the Empire State Building, suddenly appeared in the distance. The robot was so huge that I could see it from the knees up even though it was behind two-story houses and full-grown trees. Something in my brain that sounded like a radio broadcast urged everyone to get inside because there were huge robots coming to destroy everything. My brother and I ran into the garage, and I reached up to grab the garage door and pull it down. I pulled it down very slowly, and I remember distinctly noticing first the sky and the robot, then the trees, then the porch, and finally the driveway disappearing as I pulled the door down in slow motion. When the bottom of the door touched the ground, everything went to black, and there was complete nothingness. That was the end of the dream.

I can only guess at the age I was when I first had the dream: somewhere around four or five, based on the fact that my brother looked like he was 11 or 12. The dream was extremely scary. I've always thought it was my psyche's way of recording the moment when I shut the door on life and began to live only through the Good Little Girl.

I lived through the Good Little Girl for many years, because she kept me safe, and she kept me from having to feel what was going on inside. My real self only peeked out occasionally.

But when we moved to California, I started getting a little more in touch with who I was outside the box of daughter.

# Chapter 8: California, Here We Come

The problem with growing up in a dysfunctional family is that you never know life can be any other way. From a child's point of view, it's just the way the world is. And until you discover something that shows you how different life can be, you just go along figuring the world operates exactly the same way that your family did.

If we hadn't moved to California when I was fourteen, I probably would never have left St. Louis. In California, I discovered that other parts of the world differed, sometimes radically, from the community I had grown up in.

My father received an offer from his employer to move out to California for three years to work on a special project with McDonnell Douglas. He decided to take the offer, and went on ahead to start the job and find a house while my mother made the arrangements with the movers.

My dad found a marvelous house: a modern two-story with four bedrooms, sliding glass doors to the patio on the first floor, and a balcony on the second floor. My parents chose the first floor bedroom, and I got the second floor bedroom with the sliding glass doors to the balcony. For the first time, I had a bathroom all to myself, and I loved the privacy. There was so much space, and I could sit out on the balcony and sunbathe or read in the wonderful California weather. Sometimes it felt as if my parents and I not only lived on separate floors, but led separate lives, and that was a relief. There was much more room in California to be myself. I didn't feel pressure to be exactly like my parents anymore.

The culture shock was tremendous, like moving to a different planet, but it was a very pleasant planet. People were much more relaxed in California than they were in St. Louis, and we relaxed right along with them. They accepted me, they were interested in who I was, and I found a youth group that would give me the first sense of belonging to a community that I'd ever had, at least for the next three years.

That world was so different, in fact, that even though I loved it, I had trouble adjusting. One night I went to my parents, and said, "Help me forget St. Louis." It was my way of saying that all the old stuff was getting in my way, and even though I didn't express it very well, they knew what I meant. They sent me to a psychologist, a tall, lanky, comfortable man with white hair.

He would start the session sitting on the floor, as if to invite me to go ahead and be a teenager.

"How are things going?" he would say.

"Okay," I would reply, not sure whether he's asking about anything in particular.

"What would you like to talk about?"

"I don't know."

I'm sure he was good at what he did, but I had no idea how to access my feelings, let alone talk about them. I desperately wanted help, but I didn't know where to begin. I tried being the Good Little Girl, but that didn't feel right with him, and I didn't know how else to be. I saw him for a few months, and then stopped.

One of the habits I had to break when we moved to California was the "I'm sorry" habit. In St. Louis, I had learned that I could keep the peace sometimes by apologizing for everything, even before it happened. Eventually, I just said, "I'm sorry" whenever it looked like my mother was about to blow, even when I hadn't done anything, even when I didn't know *why* she might blow. It was as if I could read her mood with my DNA, and I had learned to handle her by apologizing, in hopes of defusing the situation before it got out of hand.

By the time I got to junior high school, I felt responsible for everything, even when things weren't my fault. When someone got hurt in my presence during recess, I said, "I'm sorry." When someone dropped something on the floor next to me, "I'm sorry." When I hadn't understood because someone mumbled, I apologized. I thought everything bad that happened was my fault.

Throughout my life, when I said, "I'm sorry" to my mother, she would say in a hurt tone of voice, "I'm sorry, too!" And most of the time, I hadn't intentionally done anything to hurt her; it just seemed to turn out that way. Most of the time, I was just trying to get things to work for me, to get my own needs met, but somehow whatever I did was always wrong in her eyes, and then I had to apologize. Every time she said, "I'm sorry, too!", I got nauseous. I felt like I was never, ever forgiven for any of my mistakes, and that I could never, ever do enough to make up for them. But that didn't stop me from trying.

Part of the problem was that my mother could never be wrong, so I had to take the blame for everything that went wrong, whether it was my fault or not. My mother was probably just imitating her mother, who had done the same thing. She often said that when something went wrong in her family, her mother would ask, "What did you do?" And the tone of voice my mother imitated did not sound curious. It sounded reproachful.

I remember once standing in the garage as an adult with my father, watching my mother wheel a large potted plant out of the sun into the shade. "Who left this out here?" she demanded, immediately angry at whoever had been thoughtless enough to leave the poor shade-loving plant out in the sun. Dad and I looked at each other with immediate knowing that neither one of us had done anything at all with the plant. And there was no one else there.

I never once in my whole life heard my mother say she was wrong about anything. I imagine she felt as if admitting a mistake would cause her to disintegrate. So I always felt as if anything that got messed up was my fault, even if I hadn't done anything to cause it.

One day, I was sitting in the high school cafeteria with my friend Diane, a native Californian with a very relaxed demeanor and easygoing point of view. I reached toward the middle of the table to grab a napkin from the napkin holder, and my tray bumped hers. I jumped to apologize, still fearful of making others angry.

"I'm sorry," I said, as quickly as I could. My muscles clenched. I was afraid she wouldn't be my friend any more.

"It's okay," she said. "No problem."

The habit was tenacious. "I didn't mean to bump your tray."

"Kathy, it's okay. It didn't hurt anything." She crunched a potato chip, squinted at me with a little smile, and then she said, "You know, you say 'I'm sorry' all the time. I mean, like *all the time.*"

I blinked, considering. "I do?" The habit was so automatic that I'd never even noticed.

"*All the time,*" Diane said. "You gotta stop. You sound like a four-year-old." She crunched another chip.

"Yeah," I said, looking down at my plate, feeling like a four-year-old. "Thanks. I'll work on it."

And I did. It wasn't easy, but I finally broke the habit, and in its place my psyche installed a little shoe, way up above my head, that threatened to drop on me until well past the time my parents were gone. If I didn't apologize right off the bat, my subconscious reasoned, then I needed to expect that other shoe to drop anytime, anywhere.

In college, the shoe turned into panic attacks.

But in California, I quickly became an accepted member of the youth group at church, and happily joined in their many activities. My parents had decided we would go to a Methodist church down the street instead of a Disciples of Christ church. The youth group was run by a very hip minister, Steve Cochran. He was the perfect mix of authority and friendliness, always willing to talk about what was troubling us, but able to herd us back into whatever we were supposed to be doing when needed. He totally changed my perspective on what ministers were like. I always felt comfortable around him. He was probably a great dad.

After the first service we attended, Steve came right up to me and stuck out his hand.

"Hi," he said, his comfortable, friendly grin putting me right at ease.

I took his hand. It was warm, and felt protective. "Hi."

"I'm Steve Cochran, the youth minister. Are you new to the area?"

I nodded. "We just moved here from St. Louis." He let go of my hand, and I wanted him to take it again. "I'm Kathy Mayfield."

"Nice to meet you. We have a very active youth group here. We're playing volleyball this afternoon at 2:00. Would you like to join us?"

And presto, I belonged to a group of smart, happy, active young people. They seemed so different from my peer group in St. Louis: they were welcoming, accepting, happy to meet me, and totally uncritical. We played volleyball every Sunday afternoon, and Steve played right along with us, became one of us. There was a lot of team chatter, like "Good serve!" and "Way to go!" Even though I made a lot of beginner mistakes, everyone was still supportive: "Good try!" "You'll get it next time." And eventually I did.

The easy atmosphere of nonjudgmentalism allowed me to nudge some of my shell aside, begin to enjoy participating in a group, and start to appreciate my abilities a little more. The youth group took trips several times a year, and I saw more of the world in three years than I'd seen in my whole life, from Yosemite National Park and other places in California, to Bryce Canyon and Zion National Park in Utah. We even stopped for an hour once in Las Vegas—a real thrill for a kid with who was hungry to explore the world.

My experience at school was much better than it had been in St. Louis, too. The high school was much bigger than the junior high I'd gone to in St. Louis, and had a huge plaza in the middle with plantings and a fountain, and seagulls flying across as we went from one class to another. I enjoyed being outdoors year-round. And I found a creative outlet that would teach me all about myself and life and feelings and relationships, even if it wasn't quite real. I found acting.

I had wanted to be an actor ever since I was small, and now I finally had the chance. The theater department at my high school in California had a full-fledged program that put on several major shows a year and included classes in acting, scene study, theater history, and improvisation. I felt like I had finally found my true home.

With acting, I could be a different person as I portrayed a character. I learned all about feelings—what kinds there were, how people might express them, and what they meant. I could express the feelings I had to keep under wraps at home: I could be angry without any consequences; I could cry and no one would belittle me for being "too sensitive"; I could talk back to the other characters when the script called for it; and I could show my brains when I played a brainy character. I could have a lot of different kinds of life experiences without going anywhere or putting myself in risky real-life situations. The positive attention I received from directors and other actors, and from the audience when we performed, began to seep into the dark void of sadness in my soul. Starved for that attention and encouraging feedback, I drank it up every chance I got.

I felt so free, and in the acting department I found a second community of like-minded people who accepted and supported and encouraged me, who appreciated my abilities instead of criticizing me and making me feel small. I finally learned what it felt like to belong. I became part of two more families, except that the youth group and the theater department were happy families, not families who criticized me and made me feel small.

The world of acting seemed much more functional than my family relationships, and loads more fun. I could be a drinker, a druggie, a lazy ass, a bitch, or a murderer, with no consequences whatsoever. I loved it, and I continued acting for more than 25 years.

When I wasn't working on a scene for class or rehearsing for a play, I was helping out with the props or scene painting. I got to stay out later when I went to rehearsals than I would have if I'd just gone out with friends. My parents liked the fact that I was into acting. It gave them something to be proud of me for besides my piano playing. My mother, in fact, particularly enjoyed it.

"I used to perform all the time in college," she said, standing up tall with her chest and her jaw pushed out. She intimated that she had been one of the theater professor's favorites. I always wished I could go back in time to find out whether some of her stories were actually true.

One of my favorite roles was Annie Sullivan in *The Miracle Worker*. This was my first major role, and when I got cast, the director told me, "Now, you're going to have to really take the stage here." And I did. I worked my butt off—on the lines, the character, the Irish accent—in rehearsals and on my own. I remember rehearsing the dining room scene over and over, the one where Annie and Helen fight about whether or not Helen will hold a spoon. I wish I could remember the last name of the actress who played Helen—Lia something—she was dynamite. We had bumps and bruises after rehearsals and performances, and we didn't use stage slaps. We used real ones. The role provided great physical exercise, and was very, very satisfying, like being right inside a live computer game.

Lia and I had an interesting offstage relationship—we were friendly but cool, with a current of wariness sputtering under the surface, as if the onstage relationship was so much more important, so much bigger and bolder. I discovered later that this is often true in relationships between actors. Onstage, we totally trusted each other; offstage our relationships had an air of uncertainty, as if we knew each others' characters better than we knew each others' real selves. One of the many attractions of acting is the feeling of being able to completely trust the other actors onstage, at least when you're in a production with those who are truly dedicated to acting.

The dining room scene in *The Miracle Worker* ended with both of us rolling under the table among the discarded spoons, clenching each others' hair and grunting (me) and screaming (Lia) as the lights came down. The audience always applauded after that scene, and we got standing ovations after every show. That show was a powerful experience for all of us, and I began to feel as if maybe there was something I could do well after all. I started thinking about pursuing a professional career.

By the time I was a junior, I had worked my way up from playing tiny parts to leading roles, and I felt as if I had finally found my place in life. I won the Best Actress in a Leading Role award for my performance as Annie Sullivan at the year-end banquet. In California, I finally began to discover who I was outside of the box. I found complete acceptance in two communities, I found acting, and I enjoyed a close relationship with a wonderful first love named Rob. My parents loved Rob—he was smart and polite and together. He was sweet and fun, and kind to me, and I have nothing but good memories of that relationship, especially the night on the beach when we built a small fire and cooked hot dogs, and later I lost my contact lens in his sleeping bag. Life was an adventure, I was enjoying myself, and I was learning to connect with like-minded people.

At the end of my junior year, my father's company finished the job with McDonnell Douglas, and it was time to return to St. Louis. When my parents told me we were moving back, I cried in front of them for the first time in many years, and pleaded with them to let me stay.

"I'll do anything," I promised through my tears. "I'll get a part-time job to pay for my food and clothes, I'll stay with one of your friends. Please, I really want to stay. I'll do anything."

But my parents said, "You're only seventeen. You have to go back with us."

My fate was sealed, and forever after that, I was afraid my parents could drag me back home whenever they wanted to, just like they dragged my brother back home over and over when he ran away. The apron strings attached themselves to me with superglue.

It wasn't until many, many years later that my mother told me Steve Cochran had called her and suggested that it would be better for me if they could find a way to let me stay in California. He knew enough about me to realize that I had found freedom in my life for the first time, and he cared enough to encourage my parents to do what was best for me. But my parents couldn't let me go. They still needed me too much.

When I was in my forties, my father showed me an article in the newsletter for the Institute of Electrical and Electronics Engineers, of which he was a member. One of the men he had worked with on the job for McDonnell Douglas had struck out on his own as a consultant instead of returning to St. Louis with the rest of the group when the job was finished.

"He's probably making a lot of money," my dad said grimly. And then he surprised me by saying, "It took me awhile to realize that you and Mom would have preferred to stay in California. But by that time, we had bought the house in St. Louis, and I was so close to retirement then. I would have lost my pension." I guess he was paying attention in his quiet way after all.

Sometimes I wonder if all my urges to strike out on my own and start my own business, and my aversion to working in an unrewarding job, weren't emotional leftovers from my dad. Staying at the same company for over 25 years caused him to shove all his creativity into his workshop, where he could only enjoy it on evenings and weekends. But he did get his pension. Security was very important to him. I imagine that seeing the numbers in his mutual funds rise was the only thing that made him feel safe.

In any case, late in the spring of 1975, we headed back to St. Louis.

# Chapter 9: St. Louis Blues

When we returned to St. Louis, we moved into a two-bedroom second-floor apartment in a lovely old house with a huge yard and ancient trees, just a few blocks from the house I'd grown up in, where we stayed while my parents looked for a house. The apartment was a far cry from the two-story four-bedroom with sliding glass doors and great weather that we'd had in California. We all tried to squeeze back into the selves we'd been before we moved to the coast, but it didn't work. Pandora's Box had been opened, and there was no going back. In many ways, I'm very thankful to have had the California experience: living there completely shattered the illusion I grew up with that the world operated the same way my family did.

My parents went back to the same Disciples of Christ church, where they were welcomed with open arms, while I headed to the local high school for my senior year. I was a stranger to the theater department, and the lead roles in the mainstage productions went to students who had been involved in the department since freshman year. There was no room for a newcomer. My faith in my acting ability plummeted right along with my mood. I hadn't learned yet that true confidence comes from within, not from the outside world.

Few of my friends from junior high were there, and none of them invited me into the solid cliques that had formed in my absence. There was no volleyball, and though I tried the youth group at church with high expectations, it was a real disappointment, so I didn't last long. We watched videos of missions in foreign countries and painted rooms in the church, and relationships among the leader and the young people were strained, as most relationships in St. Louis seemed to be.

When I wasn't in school, I sat in my bedroom under a smothering cloud of depression. I wrote long letters to Rob, wanting to make plans to head out to California as soon as possible to be with him. Three years older than me and on his own now, he wrote back that he missed me just as much, but that running away wasn't the answer. He suggested I finish high school, and then reconsider. I knew that was the right thing to do, but I felt as if I was disappearing into a haze of sadness and futility. After fourteen years of living in what felt like a prison in St. Louis, I had finally been set free in the world. And now I was back in prison.

I started hanging out with a couple of friends who smoked pot, and we smoked more and more as the year went on. Sadly, drugs helped me forget that life could be good, and fun, and that people could be supportive and encouraging. But they also made it easier to deny my pain and ignore the promptings of the Good Little Girl, which loosened the hold she had on me. I put headphones on to shut out the world, and listened to Alice Cooper and Black Sabbath at top volume. I stopped trying to have fun or achieve anything.

As I sank back into my old life and pushed my feelings under wraps again, I forgot what love was, what it felt like to be accepted and appreciated, and what it was like to be an integral member of a community.

In true teenager fashion, I tried a few other drugs along with pot, and started smoking cigarettes. By the end of my senior year I was totally enveloped in the safe cloud of drugs which protected me from the choking depths of depression and repressed anger. As I think about that time in my life, I realize that I probably needed to have my thoughts and feelings turned off for a few years, until I could deal with the loss of a good life newly discovered, the pain of having finally found something I had always wanted, and then having it jerked away from me again.

I went back to visit Rob over Christmas vacation that year, staying with one of the friends I'd gotten close to in California. We had a good time, but it wasn't the same. I'd already lost a large part of the self and the sense of freedom I had found in California. I was back in the box of daughter.

My parents found a nice, solid three-bedroom house a few miles away on a dead-end street, and we lived there for the last few months of my senior year. The only thing I knew for sure was that I wanted to take a year off before going to college. After being immersed in the totally different world of California for three years and then being forced to return to St. Louis, I was very bewildered. Deep down I knew that I didn't have any idea how the world worked, and I needed to figure out where I wanted to go from here. I desperately needed to sort out some of my confusion about life.

I told my parents that I wanted to take a year off before starting college to figure things out. But my mother responded, "If you don't go to college now, you'll never go," so I went ahead, knowing that I wasn't ready. Once again, what I needed didn't matter; what my mother wanted was what was most important. My drug use intensified.

Years later, my mother said, "We thought we lost you then." I imagine my drug use was fairly obvious, but my parents never confronted me about it. They were probably afraid that if they did, I would start to drift away as Michael had over the years. Then there would be no one left to keep them from fully being with each other.

The college I went to had a system of culling talent in the school, whereby a small portion of the sophomore class were not invited back for the final two years. For whatever reason, there had been an upswing in the number of students when I enrolled, so that year they ended up cutting a third of the sophomore class. I didn't make the cut.

I remember Lenny, my best friend at the time, bursting into tears when he heard I wouldn't be returning (he had been accepted). I didn't have any feelings about being cut except for the all-too-familiar feeling of having failed at something I wanted to do, of not being good enough, of being blocked once again from moving forward in my life. Only this time it wasn't my mother that blocked me. This time, it seemed the world didn't want me.

When I gave my parents the news about not making the cut and said that I was going to take a year off to find another college, they grudgingly agreed, and suggested that I get a job. So I spent the next year working first as a mail delivery person, then as a receptionist, for a paint and chemical manufacturer. I also auditioned for a couple of community theater productions, and played a couple of small roles, but by that point my life was centered around smoking pot and just making it through another day.

My mother was right. I was pretty lost.

I began to reconnect with myself the next year when I went back to college in Denver. I felt better living at a distance from my parents, and I got several good roles in those two years. Being away from my druggie friends helped as well, and by the time I graduated, I had pretty much put my drug use behind me.

I was beginning to wake up again to the possibilities in life, beginning to understand that I could live something other than the life my parents had. I had rediscovered that I could be accepted within a community of like-minded others, and as my depression lifted, I remembered that I wasn't a horrible person. I even began to believe once more that I might have some talent for acting, and I made some good friends in Denver.

But still the past haunted me, and I worried that even if I could find a way of life that I enjoyed, someone would take it away again, the way my life in California had been taken away. I hadn't gotten very much of what I'd wanted in my lifetime, and the uncertainty of my childhood had worn deep ruts in my brain and lowered my expectations.

Until I was in my fifties, every time I began to make positive changes in my life, my psyche would start insisting that what I'd found or accomplished was going to be "taken away" all over again, so in order to avoid the pain of losing what I'd gained, I unconsciously sabotaged it, or stopped trying to move forward, and sank back into the familiar and comfortable sense of futility. And when I did manage to pull myself up and start feeling positive about my life, all it took was one phone call from my mother to drag me back down. Her depression would bleed through the line and cover me like mud in a swamp.

My mother had started making jewelry with beads. She had a little stand that held the end of the wire, and she would thread the beads onto the wire as she pulled it through the loop. My father had to put the clasps on when each piece was finished, because, she said, "I can't get my fingers to go." She wanted to create so badly, and it was so unsatisfying for her because her fingers wouldn't work and she couldn't see very well. I wondered why she chose something like jewelry that was obviously so difficult and unsatisfying, given her limitations. It seemed as if she were trying to find herself, but denying herself the pleasure of self-expression, all at the same time.

I know what she was feeling. I grew up with exactly the same problem.

I tried to help, but to no avail. My mother complained to me constantly that she needed something new to focus on. And I kept trying to fix the problem every time.

"I need a new project," my mother says on the phone. Her voice is colored by a desperate note of pleading, as if her very soul is frantic for relief.

A feeling of dismay creeps into my chest as the weight of responsibility for my mother's happiness drops on me once again. "How about painting? You used to enjoy that."

"I can't hold a brush very well anymore."

I feel sorry for her, because her hands have always given her pain and kept her from doing things she wants to do.

"I saw a velvet painting last month in a craft store," I say, boosting the usually positive tone I try to take with her. "All you have to do is color in the white spaces with magic markers, and you've got a pretty picture of a kitten." That should spark some interest—my mother's passion for cats matched my own. "Want me to get you one?"

"No, don't spend your money on me."

I can never figure out how to get off this merry-go-round. Does it please her somehow to keep rejecting every idea I come up with?

Suddenly, a new idea comes to me, one that might not hurt her hands, and her poor vision wouldn't matter. "How about finger painting?"

I hold my breath, praying for the weight to be lifted, praying for her to finally find something that will make her happy, praying for us to connect around something that's positive and enjoyable.

"No, I don't think so." Her depression reverberates along the phone line, and the weight increases. I'm out of ideas, and once again there's no resolution.

Over and over again, she would say she needed something, and I would suggest this or that, or get her some new creative project for Christmas or her birthday. For years, I hunted desperately in craft stores, always hoping against hope that I could find the perfect thing that would finally make her happy, yet knowing each time that it wouldn't be enough. And it never was. The feelings of failure piled on top of each other like stones in a rockslide, until I felt like I would never do anything right.

Trying everything I could think of to make my mother happy, even though it interfered with living my own life, was preferable to living in a constant awareness of her deep and unfathomable agony, and struggling under the weight of the guilt that told me I should be able to make everything better.

But I liked Denver, and I liked the feeling of being away from my parents, and consequently I developed a little bit of immunity to the parental rubber band. Shortly before I graduated from college, I called my parents and told them I would be staying in Denver. For once, there wasn't any discussion; they just said, "Okay." They were finally ready to let me go, and I knew I couldn't return to St. Louis again, couldn't lose everything I had found a second time, or I would just crash and burn.

I found an apartment, and got a full-time job working at Center Attractions, a ticket agency for the Broadway shows and dance companies that played in Denver. I auditioned at area theaters and occasionally got cast, and though I auditioned many times at the Big Cheese, the Denver Center for Performing Arts, I never got in. Somehow, that felt very familiar.

About a year after I graduated from college, I landed a job doing singing telegrams with The Singing Bees. Performing singing telegrams is actually a tremendous training ground for an actor, because you have to gauge the atmosphere of the room within five or ten seconds, and tailor your performance to match the ambience. Is this a quiet group who just wants a bit of a laugh? Or a boisterous crowd with a few drinks under their belts? Was the person receiving the birthday/anniversary/congratulatory telegram a quiet, shy type whom I should treat gently? Or someone who loved being the center of attention and could take a few gags about age in stride? My "home schooling" in picking up what was going on under the surface with people came in really handy.

One night I went to deliver a telegram in Arvada, which at that time was a newly developed suburb that I was unfamiliar with. The client who ordered the telegram had requested "Polly" Parton, one of our standard characters. The outfit included an outrageous red-sequined pantsuit, a huge fluffy blond wig, and, naturally, a humongous padded bra. I'd added lots of mascara, bright blue eyeshadow, and fire-engine-red lipstick to complete the parody.

The subdivision was so new that there weren't many street lights, and I couldn't find the street I was looking for. I stopped at a gas station on the outskirts to ask for directions, and as I made a left out of the station, I drove right over the cement island dividing the four-lane road, because I didn't see it in the dark.

As I turned right at the next stoplight, I noticed the flashing blue lights behind me, and pulled over to the side of the road. The cop sauntered up to the car, and shined his flashlight right into my eyes. He probably thought he'd caught a drunk driver.

"May I see your driver's license?" he drawled.

"Yes, sir," I said in my best Good Little Girl voice. I got out my driver's license, and as I was handing the license to him, I realized that the photo of me on the license—thin, with brown hair and little makeup—looked nothing like me in my Polly Parton getup. My nerves started jumping, and the old fear of death wormed its way back into my brain.

The cop looked at my license, he looked at me, and his eyes almost popped. He cleared his throat.

"Do you know why I stopped you?" I imagine he was already enjoying the story he'd be able to tell after he booked me at the station.

"Yes, sir," I said as politely as I could. "I ran over the cement island in the middle of the road. I'm on my way to perform a singing telegram, and I'm unfamiliar with this area." As an afterthought, I added, "Gee, there aren't many street lights here."

"Uh-huh." I could tell he wasn't buying my story.

"I'm dressed like this for the telegram. I'm with the Singing Bees." I turned sideways to point to the bee costume—the trademark outfit for the Singing Bees—lying on the back seat. My humongous boobs bumped against the steering wheel as I turned, and I felt them slide to the side. "See the bee costume in the back seat?"

I could hear an edge of hysteria creeping into my voice, feel the Good Little Girl's desperation to fix the situation. I'd seen policemen turn into monsters on TV, like my father used to do with my brother.

He shined the flashlight on the bee suit for a moment, and then said, "Stay right here, please." He went back to his car.

He kept me waiting for twenty minutes while I'm sure he performed every possible check on me, possibly even a check for suspected prostitution, because of the red sequins and huge bazoombas. I struggled to remind myself that he wasn't my father, that he probably never hit women, and that I wasn't going to die—driving over the island was a simple mistake—but my body kept telling me I was in grave danger, and I sweated and trembled for most of the twenty minutes. Visions of national news coverage of me spending the night in jail dressed as Polly Parton flashed through my head, and I thought about what my mother would say:

"I told you it wasn't a good idea to do those singing telegrams," even though she never had. "I knew you'd get in trouble."

But I've always been a good driver, and my Good Little Girl training made me into a stellar citizen in spite of my years of smoking pot, so I didn't have any kind of record. I guess the cop believed me, because he let me go with a warning, and I went off to play Polly.

Meanwhile, I started to get acting roles here and there, and I ended up spending six years in Denver "getting experience on the boards," as they say in the acting business. I played my second favorite role, Arlene in *Getting Out*, at the Mercury Café Theater, and began getting leading roles in Shakespeare productions: Viola in *Twelfth Night*, Rosalind in *As You Like It*. I was very comfortable with the classics, and enjoyed performing Shakespeare very much.

What I loved most about acting was the exploration of different characters. After a very rigid, narrow childhood, I finally got a chance to discover different aspects of myself by temporarily living other people's lives.

One of the most unusual and enjoyable roles I played was the Dwarf in a play called *Caverns* at the Changing Scene Theater. The play took place in a cave where four high school friends met for a reunion several years after graduation. The Dwarf was a creature which represented the psychological energy of the friends, the twists and turns of their relationships, the bumps and ascents and descents of the life paths they were on.

I was dressed in a gnarly black wig and brown painted burlap, with brown and black makeup smeared on my face and hands, and I took my place onstage, curled up like a rock, before the audience entered the theater. I had to lie there, barely breathing, for twenty minutes while the audience wandered in and sat down.

As the lights came up to begin the show, I would jump up from my rock position and start careening around the stage, to the inevitable gasps of the audience who had thought I was just one more piece of the set. I didn't speak until the very end of the show, but the role demanded that I be onstage almost all the time, acting out the other characters' thoughts and feelings the way an animal would, grunting and snuffling to express the emotional through-line. The role was an incredible opportunity for an actor, and it brought up an almost primordial energy from within that I hadn't known existed in me. It was an odd but extremely effective antidote to the Good Little Girl, allowing me to express every emotion there was, completely uninhibitedly. That role in particular had a very balancing effect on my psyche.

In 1983, I met my future husband, Jeff, who was an actor as well. We married in 1984, moving to New York the following spring. With expectations of great success fueled by our on-the-boards experience in Denver, we set about finding day jobs and pursuing acting careers. We began taking acting classes and going to auditions, and I got a part-time job as a legal proofreader at a major corporate law firm.

I enjoyed living in New York: the energy and diversity allowed me to gobble up chunks of life I'd missed in childhood. But acting is an incredibly tough and demanding profession. The competition is horrendously intense in New York City. There were literally hundreds of actresses my age, who looked like me and came from the Midwest to try their hand at becoming stars. Going to auditions meant getting up at 5 am to get ready and get in line by 6:30 so I could get an audition slot, sometimes after performing or rehearsing until 10 or 11 the night before. Most auditions attracted anywhere between three hundred and a thousand or more actors, depending on the project. And much of the time, we'd wait in line for hours just to file through with our best actor smiles and shake someone's hand as we gave them our photos.

Over the twelve-year period that I lived in New York, I played roles in several Off-Broadway and Off-Off-Broadway shows, as well as a few indie films, including Hal Hartley's first film, *The Unbelievable Truth*, which was shot largely in his hometown on Long Island. He went on to make several popular films, and I enjoyed working with him very much. I also played some small roles—under-fives and day players—on one of the soaps, the now defunct *Guiding Light*.

I was surviving, even thriving, in the Big Apple, and I was getting work as an actor. I was finally starting to grow some self-esteem. But every time I called my parents or went to visit, my confidence shrank again.

> "I have an audition tomorrow for the soap opera *Guiding Light*," I tell my mother on the phone. I'm proud and excited. It's not easy to get an audition for a soap, and roles on the soaps are coveted by many actors. Not only does the work pay very well, but the atmosphere is totally professional, the actors are treated with great respect, and it's an opportunity to delve deeply into a character over a long period of time.
>
> My mother is an avid watcher of *As the World Turns*, so I figure she'll be thrilled. I hold my breath, waiting for her yelp of excitement. "That's nice," she says. "I finished another afghan."
>
> My chest closes, and my pride whirls away into nothingness. Since we're obviously not going to talk about whatever is going on in my life, there's only one thing left to do. "What color?" I ask, the deadness spreading out from my center to numb my hands and feet.
>
> "Brown and pink. It looks prettier than it sounds," my mother says, as if to apologize. "You can see it next time you come. When are you coming to visit?"
>
> For the next 24 hours, instead of feeling confident and strong about the audition, about my acting, about myself and my life, I end up thinking about my mother and wondering why she never wants to hear what I'm doing, why she

doesn't even want to know who I am, and why those damned afghans are so important. And I think about how I should visit because she wants me to, even though I regress to a helpless, childlike state every time I go. I know that if I decide to be strong and tell her no, she'll just keep asking, badgering me until I give in and make the plane reservation. I get stuck back in the box of daughter, and I can't seem to find my way out.

I didn't get the role.

The next time we talk on the phone, she asks, "How did your audition go?"

I feel even worse about failing because I have to admit it to her. "I didn't get the role."

"Well, don't feel bad. I imagine there are a lot of actresses who are better than you are. Maybe you'd feel better if you came for a visit."

I want to bang my head against a wall.

Though I got some work as an actor during those years, I wasn't "moving up through the ranks" to better roles at better theaters the way I wanted to, and I wasn't getting any closer to supporting myself with my career. As time went on, facing the recurring rejection reminded me more and more of childhood. Unable to achieve the success I had hoped for in New York, I noticed the old feelings of failure beginning to creep back in. Talking with my mother usually helped to move the process along.

And after seven years, my marriage wasn't going well, either. Even though I truly believed that marriage should be a partnership of equals, I had unconsciously turned myself back into the Good Little Girl when we married, trying to please Jeff with everything I did, as I'd done with my mother. We had money difficulties, compounded by the fact that we were both actors with day jobs, and when I eventually figured out that I needed to take care of myself as well as taking care of Jeff, the marriage started to fall apart. We had grown in different directions.

In 1990, in an effort to understand why life was always so difficult for me, I started therapy. I knew something was wrong with my life, and I wasn't sure any more that it was me, but I didn't know what the problem could be. In therapy, I began picking at the knots in my psyche and digging underneath the corroded crust that covered the ugly story of my childhood. I had no idea how much debris I'd have to paw through before I could begin to see things clearly, but I made a start and kept plowing through the rubble until the light of truth began to shine.

Eventually, I began to realize that what was hidden inside of me was not weakness, deficiency, and incompetence, but rather a mountain of buried treasure that would immeasurably enrich my life as I found the courage to uncover and express it.

# Chapter 10: The Great Discovery

In therapy, I began to unravel the miasma that was the dysfunction of my family. Many mornings when I woke, my first thought was, "No, not consciousness. I don't want to be conscious and remember all this stuff." It was excruciating to face some of those early experiences as they surfaced from the depths of my psyche, and my therapist provided exceptional support and encouragement as I dug my way into the past.

In her book, *Tears and Tantrums*, Dr. Aletha Solter writes,

> If children are shown love and approval only when they are smiling and happy, they will learn to deny and repress a part of themselves in order to please adults. Their deepest emotions will eventually feel unacceptable, even to themselves. Without full acceptance of their feelings and emotional expressions...children cannot grow up with high self-esteem. (p. 23)

As a child, I had unwittingly created the Good Little Girl persona and repressed my feelings because the expression of emotion was unacceptable to my parents. But in therapy, I learned that it was okay to feel my feelings, that in fact they are the most accurate guide to living the life I truly want. I may not choose to act on every feeling, but when I'm able to be aware of them, I know I'm in touch with my deepest self. I also learned how important it was to express old, repressed emotions as they emerged from my unconscious, whether the feelings came through tears or anger. I discovered that each time I allowed my emotions an outlet, I felt better afterwards, and as time went by, my clarity about myself, my life, and my family grew.

In an effort to gain some distance from my past, when I was in my thirties I changed the spelling of my name to Kathi, and started journaling to stay in touch with my feelings, to record the insights that flowed up from my subconscious as part of my healing work. I found that if I didn't record the insights I had about my family, they would sink back into unconsciousness, and I would slip back into the old, familiar patterns.

I went through an extreme depression in the course of the early therapy work, and though I never made actual suicide plans, I was truly grateful for the presence of my cat. The responsibility of caring for her, and the unconditional love she offered, gave me a reason to go on.

Jeff and I divorced in 1993, and my mother told me then that Aunt Mae had been married once in the 1920s before she met and married Uncle John. Apparently there had been some kind of problem, because Aunt Mae went to her family shortly after she was married and told them that she had made a mistake. They helped her get a divorce, which was very unusual at that time. Finding out that she had been divorced made me feel better about my own decision.

I began to discover in therapy that some of the reasons I'd chosen acting as a career were related to my dysfunctional upbringing. As an actor, I was hoping to find the attention and respect I had never received from my parents. And although I enjoyed acting immensely, it was problematic in that I was using my career as a substitute for living my real life, for finding other ways to meet my emotional needs. My acting career allowed me to express my emotions freely, but I still couldn't do that in the rest of my life. Acting helped me feel competent and respected, but when I wasn't acting, I felt inept and defective all over again.

During rehearsals and performances, I enjoyed intimate and satisfying connections with other actors, both onstage and off, and I got lots of attention—usually very positive—from people in the audience. But when I wasn't acting, my depression worsened, because I wasn't living any kind of a fulfilling life—my career only made it *look* like I was, and then only when I was performing.

When I wasn't involved in a show or film, it was all I could do to trudge through my life, auditioning desperately in the hopes of getting cast so that I could feel like I was worthy again, feel like life was worth living again. I knew a number of other actors who lived with this same disparity between life and career, and I began to see how dysfunctional it could be. I started paying close attention to the ways in which the difficulties inherent in the acting business were similar to some of the patterns in my family.

Acting provided a very familiar sensation of moving back and forth between façade and reality. When I realized how perfectly acting reflected my family's pattern of behaving one way in public, and another in private, I looked around for a book that might help me cope with the problem. In spite of the huge numbers of self-help books out there, there were none specifically for actors related to the acting profession. So I decided to write one. I loved writing, and had been journaling for several years, and suddenly, trying my hand at a different kind of art seemed very appealing.

In 1996, *Smart Actors, Foolish Choices* was published by Back Stage Books. I had begun a new career.

As I began to move into writing, my mother tried to get there first and be the biggest. She started writing devotionals for the local church. Every time I mentioned something about my writing projects, she jumped in and took over the conversation, going on and on about how everyone loved her devotionals. She made it seem as if her devotionals were more important than my writing career, and she applauded her own success and belittled mine. Every time I spoke with her about writing, I got a little smaller. My feelings of competence as a writer seesawed back and forth between pride in my accomplishments and dismal feelings of failure for not achieving more success.

Occasionally, out of the blue, my mother would offer a spark of support or encouragement, just enough to keep me hungry for more: "You can do it!" Once, she even had one of my poems framed, and gave it to me for my birthday. But I couldn't let my guard down and take it in, because she was so good at striking when my guard was down. She was always able to knock me off my center—and even when she didn't, I was braced in case she did.

I was growing increasingly disenchanted with New York, and when I realized that I could be a writer without living in New York, I moved to Massachusetts in 1997. My parents came to visit shortly after I moved, bringing some furniture and dishes that they had saved for me over the years. Throughout my adult life, whenever I moved to a new place or a new space, my parents came to visit within weeks of my move—without an invitation—as if to mark their territory, to lay their claim on me and my life all over again. Nonetheless, I looked forward to a new life in a new place, to creating a wonderful writing career.

For the next several years, I pursued my writing career while I worked part-time as an editor and proofreader to support myself. I published another book on the acting business, *Acting A to Z*, and sold some articles here and there, but I couldn't seem to get very far in terms of building a real writing career. My doormat status was continually reinforced by my parents, and I imagine that I was still afraid to outdo them, to achieve any kind of success that I could call my own.

A few years after I moved to Massachusetts, my mother threw a party for me on one of my visits, inviting their friends and people in the church that I'd known since I was small. I thought she just wanted an excuse to have a party, but when I saw the cake, I started shaking. The cake itself was lovely, but my mother had scrawled "Welcome home, Kathi!" in dark blue across the light blue frosting. She was apparently hoping that, since I was no longer acting and hadn't remarried, I might decide I'd seen enough of the world, and move back "home" to St. Louis.

That incident brought back memories of the Bunny Cake birthday party on my seventh birthday, and my psyche began cheerfully tossing repressed memories and old feelings into my conscious mind, in hopes of clearing the way for more functional relating. I experienced spontaneous sessions of tears and anger when I journaled, as wounds I'd never healed and feelings I'd never faced popped up, pleading for release. I discovered that the psyche truly does want to heal itself, and it knows exactly how to do that. All I needed to do was to let it lead me where it wanted to go, be an empathic witness, and record my impressions and insights so they didn't drop back into unconsciousness.

After I came home from that trip, I told my therapist about the Bunny Cake. When I finished the story, she was silent for a moment, blinking thoughtfully, as she put together all the incidents I'd told her about over the last few years. Then she came up with the greatest idea I'd ever heard—an idea which radically changed my life and my view of myself forever.

"Have you ever thought about the possibility that your mother might have Borderline Personality Disorder?" my therapist asked.

"No," I said. "What is it?"

Her brief explanation made it seem like my mother might in fact have BPD, and when I researched the disorder online, all kinds of bells started ringing. Everything I read was a simultaneous breath of fresh air and heavy clunk of recognition.

> I love to search for things online, to have my questions answered with no argument or interruption or frenzied change of subject.
> I squint at the computer screen in the darkened room. I've hit pay dirt.
> *"People with BPD alternate between seeing themselves, and others, as either worthless or flawless."* I feel myself nodding.
> *"Their moods can swing from one extreme to the other, often within minutes."* My heart starts to beat faster. Maybe there truly is a reason my life has been so weird.
> *"They have no sense of self, and feel ignored when they are not the focus of attention."* That one hits my stomach, as I realize how right on target this is.
> *"They may even do or say something inappropriate in order to get the focus of attention back on themselves."* My breath catches in my chest. That was my mother right there.
> *"They can be verbally abusive toward people they know very well, while putting on a charming front for others, and they can switch from one mode to another within seconds."* Yes, yes, yes. I'm almost crying, it's so familiar.
> *"They often change their expectations in such a way that the other person feels they can never do anything right."* My mother was an expert on that one.
> I run for the Kleenex.

My therapist suggested I read a book called *Understanding the Borderline Mother*, and sure enough, my mother jumped out at me from every page. Suddenly, I began to understand that my mother wasn't *trying* to hurt me. She wasn't ignoring my needs because she was malicious or because I was worthless. She didn't cut me down and confuse me on purpose; it was all a result of how she saw the world, what she felt inside. Something was broken within her psyche, and that's what caused her to behave the way she did. Sympathy began to bloom in my heart, alongside the pain.

Furtively, as if somehow my mother would know what I was doing, I read everything relating to BPD that I could get my hands on. I began to feel an incredible sense of relief seeping into my bones, and my heart, accompanied by the words, "Not my fault. It wasn't my fault."

Everything that had gone wrong in my childhood—from my relationship with my mother, to food that spilled, to people who didn't cooperate—had always felt like my fault. Suddenly, there might be a reason why my relationship with my mother was so difficult.

I had always assumed that *I* was the problem. Finding out that my mother might have BPD offered a growing sense of hope that maybe I wasn't such a horrible, defective person after all. That one comment from my therapist changed my life forever. As much as I dislike putting labels on people, and even though my mother was never diagnosed, that particular label gave me the freedom to heal, to discover that I might be able to trust other people, to begin to believe in myself. I finally understood how dysfunctional my mother's behavior and her treatment of me had always been.

Armed with my new information, hearing my mother's side of a story suddenly became more interesting. I was curious as to what the Bunny Cake incident was all about, so the next time I visited, I got my mother to start reminiscing about our early family life so that my question wouldn't seem too abrupt. I didn't want to make her suspicious.

She loved being the center of attention, so she talked about this and that, and after she had been going awhile, I summoned my courage.

> Swallowing my trepidation and ignoring my body's insistent replaying of old feelings, I ask her, "Do you remember the bunny cake you made for my birthday one year?"
>
> She perks up and her eyes go hard. "Oh, yes," she says. "I remember. I worked for *three hours* putting that bunny cake together, and all any of you could say was, 'Oh, a bunny cake.'" Her voice

rises, and a bit of a sneer creeps in. "You were all so much more interested in the presents than the cake." Then she sniffed loudly, which was her way of sticking her nose in the air, and changed the subject quickly.

With a flash of insight, I realized that the cruel party game, and her enjoyment of our fear, was her retribution for our lack of appreciation for the cake. And then I knew she must have had her reasons for the other inexplicable experiences of retribution in my childhood.

After that, when I visited or spoke with my mother on the phone, I listened more carefully to her than I had in years. I was so used to the way she behaved that it had always seemed normal to me, but now I was viewing her behavior from a completely different perspective. I felt thud after thud of recognition as I began to notice how many of the things she did and said seemed odd in comparison to most people I knew. For one thing, I was always surprised when people didn't interrupt me, because my mother often did. If the conversation wasn't to her liking, she would interrupt with a whole new subject, sometimes right in the middle of a sentence.

As I started paying more attention to our interactions, I realized that because my mother consistently interrupted me, I thought other people had no interest in what I had to say. Her interruptions were so familiar that I'd never even noticed how rude her behavior was. I had always just assumed the things I said were so pathetic that no one wanted to hear them.

Our relationship had been a lifelong game of Follow the Leader, with my mother always in front. No matter what I accomplished, she needed to be bigger than I was, to remain in command. Whenever I started talking about my life, she inevitably moved right in and told me how things were going with hers, cementing my status as second-class citizen. And because I grew up with that inferior status, I automatically took it on in relationships with other people—until I found out about BPD. My new knowledge cleared the fog from my eyes so that I could see how different my mother was from most other people, how detrimental our relationship had been to my own development, and how it might be possible to interact with other people in much more satisfying ways.

Finding out about BPD allowed my psyche to begin to make sense of the puzzle that was my childhood. Insights flowed like water down a hill as I began to examine my mother's behaviors more closely and ferret out which parts of my self-image were direct results of her more dysfunctional behaviors.

As the new insights flooded my psyche, I began to see that I wasn't the person I had always thought I was. I saw that I had been performing a role, living in a box of my mother's making—whether unintentional or not—and I began to believe that if I kept digging down, deeper and deeper into my inner self, I might find something worthwhile there after all.

A major turning point in my life occurred when I picked up Alice Miller's book, *The Drama of the Gifted Child*. For the first time, I began to comprehend how terribly dysfunctional my relationship with my parents had always been, and to understand that if I pulled on the threads of what I felt inside and brought them out where I could truly see them, I would discover the truth about my childhood. I had never even considered the idea that my parents could be flawed. Most children don't, until the flaws are staring them right in the face. Reading Alice Miller's books helped me to recognize that my feelings of sadness and anger were an honest response to my parents' distorted way of relating to me, and that I wasn't defective after all. I devoured one book after another, and insights continued to flood my awareness, breaking down the fortress of my illusory deficiency.

As I looked back, I realized that I'd always suspected that something was wrong in our family, even as a child, but I had pushed that awareness into my unconscious along with everything else because I didn't have any proof. I had always known, on some deep level, how twisted everything was. But since I hadn't been able to substantiate my knowing as a child, I turned all of it on myself, and it became twisted into a belief that I was the one who was defective. Because my parents always acted as if they were right, no matter what, the only possible answer in my child's mind as to why everything seemed so messed up was that something was wrong with me.

As I slowly let go of the idea that I was deficient and incompetent, I started growing some self-esteem and feeling better about myself as I worked to understand my parents' behavior and release the past. I developed some satisfying friendships, and began to enjoy my life more. But as my parents aged, it became more and more difficult to keep my focus on my own life and the growth process I was immersed in. I felt as if I had one foot in my own life, and one in my parents'. Not only did they became more and more needy as they got older, they criticized me more often as they tried to cope with the inevitable loss of strength and increase in imperfection that is often part of the aging process. As they grew weaker, they had to work much harder at denying their difficulties and shoring up the façade of perfection, and they accomplished that by cutting me down so that I seemed even weaker than they did. So the more I tried to grow and strengthen my sense of self-worth, the more they hammered at me.

The belittling was constant, and came from both sides.

"Pull in your tummy!"

"This light is too bright. Why don't you use 40-watt bulbs? They're cheaper."

"You need some new clothes. That looks sloppy."

"Aren't you supposed to use cold water when you're cleaning the tub?"

"Do you have to buy bottled water? Can't you just boil it?"

I wanted to tell them to leave me alone. I wanted to release the volcanic accumulation of anger that had been building for decades, but my parents were coiled so tightly with their own anger and frustration at life that part of me was still afraid one of them would go over the edge, and I would die. I tried to stand up for my own point of view, hoping that at least the criticism would stop. But they criticized me even more. They just weren't going to let me win a single point. They wanted me to stay right in the box they had built for me.

By this time, intellectually I knew exactly what my parents were doing—putting me down so that they could feel powerful—and I knew that my view of myself was distorted by the years of abuse. But because I had been so forcefully trained for so many years, their behavior still had the desired effect of planting the seeds of doubt in my mind.

Though I tried as hard as I could to be successful with everything I did, my neural network still went right along with my parents, believing the picture they painted of who I was. I struggled fervently to move forward, to ferret out the dysfunction, to build my self-esteem and see the relationship more clearly, and I gained ground inch by hard-won inch.

Even though I had achieved a lot of clarity about how dysfunctional and enmeshed our relationship was, I still had trouble creating a strong sense of self. Every time I visited, every time I talked with them, simply being in their presence or hearing their voices and responding to the old dysfunctional cues smothered me with my childhood perspective, and I lost my way over and over again.

When I didn't have contact with my parents for a few days, my depression lifted, and I pursued my writing with gusto. I went out with friends; I felt like my life was moving forward again. But as soon as I spoke with my parents, I felt dragged back into the dismal pit of despair, trying once again to fight my way out of the box. With my therapist's help, each time I ended up back in the box, it became easier to break out and see myself from my own perspective.

There was no one else my parents could criticize. My brother had decided several years earlier that he didn't want to relate to them any longer—and I didn't blame him—so they had no contact with him. Their other relatives were either gone or lived far away. So I was the only family member they had left. As horrible as our relationship became toward the end, it just didn't seem fair to abandon my parents in their old age. And I had enough love left for both of them that I wasn't willing to commit the cruelty of leaving them totally on their own.

Though I resisted the imperatives of the Good Little Girl role, as someone with a healthy dose of compassion and a deep connection to heart and spirit, I struggled powerfully with the need to do the best I could for my parents while still trying to grow and move my life forward. I fought the passionate urge to fling the energy of my own anger back at them, but with the burning memory of my mother's anger still in my nerves, I couldn't bring myself to do that.

As I endeavored to deepen my spiritual life, I teetered back and forth between feeling like a Goody Two Shoes for not expressing my anger at them, and being angry at myself for allowing myself to be a dumping ground for the depression and angst they were experiencing in their struggles with aging. The fact that I had tried so hard to overcome my Good Little Girl training made it more difficult to accept and act from my own inner sense of honor and integrity, my real desire to be a good person and do what was right.

I knew my parents were suffering, and I wanted to alleviate their pain in any way I could. But I was desperate to grow and explore, to create a fulfilling and productive life for myself. For the next several years, I swung in and out of the box of daughter like a jack-in-the-box on a caffeine high.

# Chapter 11: We're All Connected

By the time I was in my forties, you'd think I'd have managed to get some emotional distance from my parents, or at least be able to set some limits on my commitment to continue having contact with them. But the more I tried to set limits with them, the more they wanted to talk on the phone and have me visit, and when I visited, I had a hard time getting any time at all to myself. My mother commandeered my attention most of the time, and when I finally managed to get away to take a short break, my father would step in with his graphs and investment ideas.

I know that our relationship wouldn't have been nearly as difficult if our interactions were mutually beneficial, but my parents seemed to have no interest in any of my thoughts or feelings or ideas or projects. They didn't ask me about my life anymore; they only wanted me to listen to them and agree with them. They needed constant attention, and they wanted me to provide all of it.

I know they just wanted some kind of connection, and I know they were lonely. I wanted a connection, too, but the kind of heart-to-heart connection I wanted wasn't something they could relate to. Eventually, it took so much of my energy to relate to them that I stopped wanting any kind of connection, and started trying to avoid it. I closed myself down, as I had when I was a child. One day, my father said, "You don't say much about what's going on in your life." It was safer that way.

I provided as much attention for my parents as I could without screaming or going insane, but it was never enough. They always wanted more, more, more. The bathroom was the only escape when I went to visit them. Sometimes I screamed silently in there.

I felt like a fly in a spider's web.

I found an absolutely clear and perfect definition of what it was like in Martha Beck's amazing book, *Steering by Starlight*. Ms. Beck calls the kind of love I shared with my parents "Spider Love":

If you went into your garden, recruited a spider, and asked it, "What do you love most?" the spider might answer, "I love flies." This is true. Spiders enjoy a tasty fly the way I enjoy ice cream. And how does this love cause a spider to behave? Well, it makes a sticky web, catches flies alive, wraps them up to keep them from escaping, and keeps them there, conscious but helpless. Then, whenever the spider needs a snack, it scurries over to the fly, injects it with venom to dissolve some of its insides, and slurps up some of its life force.

This is the way many people think of "love." They will say, in all honesty, that they love their children, their partners, their friends more than anything in the world. But their love is *consumptive*, not giving. They need their "loved ones" to feed them emotionally, so they imprison people, trap them in webs of obligation or guilt, paralyze them to keep them from going away. They love other people the way spiders love flies. (p. 196-7)

When I read Ms. Beck's words, I wanted to slump to the floor and never get up. I felt incredibly validated. She had described exactly how I felt for most of my life, in my obligation of being "the fly" for my parents. I had learned as a child to let myself be used by them because I didn't know life could be any other way.

One day, I was sitting in my therapist's office, and she brought up the issue of boundaries.

"What's a boundary?" I asked.

I had no idea that I could set limits on what I would accept in terms of another person's behavior. I didn't know that many people learn how to set boundaries as children—probably by example as much as by trial and error—and that most of the time when a person sets a boundary, people will respect it. The whole concept was completely foreign to me.

I learned that boundaries tell us where we end and another person begins. Since my mother treated me as an extension of herself, I saw myself that way, and until I went into therapy, I never learned to separate her behavior and her view of who I was from how I saw myself.

With my therapist's help, I learned that I could set limits on my mother's behavior. For instance, if she asked when I was coming to visit, I could assertively state, "Not until Christmas." The only problem was, my mother ignored all of the boundaries I tried to set, as she had when I was small. She couldn't understand that I might want something different than she wanted. So she would hammer me with various renditions of "When are you coming to visit?" until it was just easier to give in and go. And of course, that technique was exactly what had kept me from learning about boundaries in the first place.

With most other people, when I set a boundary, it was respected.

By this time, because I knew how dysfunctional my relationship with my parents was, almost every interaction with them made me feel sick. But even though my relationship with them sickened me, I couldn't stop. The burden of guilt dragged me under whenever I tried to separate, and I was culturally bound by duty as a daughter to see to their needs. Though I knew intellectually that I should have the power to make choices in my life, the feeling that if I didn't do what they wanted I might end up dying was always subconsciously in my way. They were incredibly strong, dynamic people, and the old fear was lodged deep in my psyche like a festering splinter. I simply couldn't cut off my relationship with them.

It was like walking into a spider web in the woods: once it's touched you, it's difficult to get it all off. I was always exhausted after getting off the phone with them or after returning from a visit with them, and each time it took longer to recover. My health was slowly declining, and other than attributing more aches and pains and tired days to aging, I didn't notice the downhill glide until it was almost too late.

It got a little easier to hold my ground when I was in my late forties, because they were in their late eighties, and beginning to weaken just a bit, and by that time I had had enough therapy that I could finally trust myself to be fairly sure of what was true and what wasn't.

On one of my visits, we're trying to decide where to go for dinner. My mother wants Chinese; my father wants Mexican. I want to go somewhere else, just so neither of them spoils dinner by being angry that they didn't get their way. So I suggest the Olive Garden, which has garnered favorable reviews from everyone at one time or another. The wrangling about where to go is making me crazy, so I go hide in the bathroom for a few minutes.

When I come out, my parents are still arguing, their bodies pointed toward each other in mental combat, each of them desperately needing to control the situation in order to feel okay about themselves. And yet the language is still faintly polite, the ingrained politeness being the only thing that's standing in the way of all-out war. By this time, neither of them cares where we eat, they just want to win the battle.

"I thought we decided to go to the China Buffet," my mother insists. Her body is vibrating with tension, with the need to win.

"No, honey, we didn't," my father huffs. His feet are planted, his arms stick-straight. In their later years, he had learned how to stand up to my mother, because years before, his habit of giving in had landed him in the emergency room with a major ulcer attack.

"But Kathi said she wanted Chinese!" my mother says in desperation, swinging her head towards me with pleading eyes as I slide into the room from the bathroom.

"No, I didn't," I say, speaking clearly and distinctly so no one can mistake my words. "I suggested the Olive Garden."

My mother is caught in the lie. This time she can't deny what I'm saying, because all three of us know I'm telling the truth. But she doesn't apologize, or even acknowledge it; she just says, "Well, I guess I can get the shrimp pasta."

I suddenly saw with excruciating clarity exactly what was going on when each of them tried to get me to side with them. Partly, they enjoyed having an audience for their verbal wrestling matches. And I imagine their arguments made life feel exciting again, especially with an audience watching. But mostly, they each wanted a pawn in the battle in order to pull more of the power over to their side. The spiders were fighting over the fly. Whoever could control me would become the leader on the side of two-against-one. Whoever lost was odd man (or woman) out.

It was sickening to think that they probably saw me as a pawn instead of a person. And oddly enough, that's exactly what I felt like most of the time.

Sometimes I don't know how I made it through those last years. I just kept going to therapy and journaling and working to figure it all out, and trying to let it all go so I could keep it from infecting my relationships with other people in my life.

Along with therapy, I devoured Alice Miller's wonderful books, John Bradshaw's books on healing shame, and piles of other books on toxic parents, dysfunctional families, and coping with narcissists. Philip Greven's book, *The Protestant Temperament*, explained a great deal of our family dysfunction in relation to religion, especially his statement that "Evangelical parents were engaged in war with their children, a war which could end only with total victory by the parents and unconditional surrender by the child" (p. 37). I read everything I could get my hands on about family systems, and when I found a tiny thread from childhood to unravel, I pulled on it gently to see where it would lead, and invariably came up with a whole spool by the time I figured a piece of the pattern out.

I realize now that it wasn't just daughterly duty that bound me to my parents. And it wasn't simply the old fear that they could drag me back at any time the way they'd yanked me out of the good life I'd set up in California. I couldn't break away because I wasn't ready to face my own feelings of disgust, the sickening codependent mélange of love and hate for the people who had kept me emotionally captive, who attempted to control my actions, my beliefs, my values, and my life, even while they presented a façade of being good and helpful. It's even harder to face all those feelings when one has always been a Good Little

Girl. This time, *I* felt like the monster.

Most of all, I couldn't separate from my parents because of the terrible physical and psychic discomfort I experienced when I tried. I wanted desperately to separate mentally and emotionally years before they passed away, but when I ignored their calls or put off visiting too long, I could feel their need and their displeasure growing and growing, even a thousand miles away. I felt like my nerves were being pulled out through my pores when it happened, and it got worse and worse the longer I ignored them. So I would finally give in and call or visit, just to get some relief physically. I still don't know how they did that.

But however they did it, my parents knew how to burrow into my psyche, even when they were 1,000 miles away. Whether it was a form of family telepathy, or quantum entanglement with my DNA, they knew exactly how to manipulate my puppet strings.

When I was 45, I was wandering around Home Depot one day, making plans and taking notes for materials I needed to refinish a pantry in my house. I was having a good day; I felt fine, and I was looking forward to finishing the project. I took a restroom break, and when I walked out of the restroom, suddenly the store was way too big, there was way too much stuff in there, and all I wanted to do was get out of there and go home. I couldn't figure out what happened.

When I got home, I discovered a message from my parents on the answering machine. They had called just about the time I went to the restroom in Home Depot. They *wanted* me, and though I didn't know at the time what was causing my distress, I *felt* it, and it yanked me right out of what I was doing.

For most of my life, I've known what was going on with other people under the surface. I've always been an "emotional sponge," unintentionally soaking up other people's feelings. Sometimes I suddenly became angry or sad for no reason, and I eventually realized I was picking up other people's emotions. Many times, I didn't know which of the feelings were my own and which might be my parents' or other people's. I wondered if my sensitivity could have been a result of the blast of electricity I'd received as a child when I sucked on my father's razor cord. And as my parents aged, I felt their emotions more strongly and more often. It was a huge distraction.

All of my life, I had felt my mother in my nerves, in my brain, in my belly, even when she wasn't with me. I could feel the ebb and flow of her anger and depression, and in my adult years, the terrible struggle she was having with the aging process. I couldn't disconnect. She scrabbled her way in through my pores. I felt as if I had never grown any skin, and lived with my nerves sitting right out on the surface of my body, waiting to be plucked.

When I read about the discovery that mother and child exchange cells during gestation, and carry those cells within their bodies throughout their lives, I wasn't at all surprised.

Over the years, I've met many other people who've had the same kinds of experiences I have, who go through life soaking up other people's emotions. I believe that emotions are a form of energy, just like thoughts are, and that they radiate a force which sensitive people pick up if the emotion is not dealt with by the person to whom it belongs. I am what Michael Jawer and Marc Micozzi call a "thin-boundary person" in their groundbreaking book, *The Spiritual Anatomy of Emotion*.

Even though I was fighting my way into a more functional perspective and desperately trying to leave the past behind, I still felt compelled to go see my parents every year or so, just so my mother would stop haranguing me about visiting. Each time, within minutes of being with them, my mother took over, and I got locked into the old role, the box of Good Little Girl that kept me protected.

Once I had managed to escape the web after a visit and go home, it would take me weeks to shake off the willies and settle myself in my life again. Within a few months my mother would be haranguing me once more: "When are you coming to visit?" And she would ask again every few weeks, growing more and more insistent, until I couldn't stand it anymore, and finally gave in and made a plane reservation.

Practically every time I went to visit, my mother would badger me for weeks beforehand to agree to play a piano concert for the residents. I'd like to think that she was proud of me, but my gut instinct is that she was motivated more by the enthusiastic comments she told me she received from people for weeks afterwards.

In my late forties, I'd been dabbling in composing, and with my parents and a few of the residents in attendance at a concert in the lounge, I announced that I wanted to play a piece I had composed. I'd already received appreciation for it back home in Massachusetts, and I wanted to share something of my heart that I'd created.

As I finished the piece, my mother appeared at the entrance to the room with her walker, holding a couple of pages of music in her hand. She hobbled over to me as the residents applauded, handed me the music, and said, "Would you play this? I've wanted to hear it for so long." Apparently my mother couldn't stand the thought of my doing something she had never done, and so not only did she leave the room while I was playing and withhold any comment at all, she forced the focus of attention back to herself by giving me a piece of her choice to play. A little more slurping of the fly's life force energy.

In that moment, I realized how ceaselessly she had always put me down in order to make herself feel bigger and better. And as a result of that insight, I was able to forgive myself for what I had always thought were shameful failures in my life, because I finally understood on a gut level that they weren't entirely my fault.

Later, one of the other residents told me how much she had enjoyed the piece I composed. She pulled me aside while my mother was talking with someone else. "It was very lovely," she told me. I almost cried with happiness that someone had appreciated it.

Years later, my father had an interesting response to another piece I composed.

"That's pretty!" he said. "What was that?"

"It's one of the pieces I composed," I said, with just a smidgen of pride.

He was silent for a moment, his face a mask. "Oh," he said, sounding mildly disappointed. "I guess that's where I've heard it." And he turned his walker around and ambled off.

After many years of going to visit for a week and coming home totally exhausted, one year I decided to make the reservation for five days instead of a week. I knew that would be all I could stand. I still remember the outrage in my mother's voice when I told her I'd only be visiting for five days. She barked, "That's not long enough!" But it was more than enough for me, and I managed to stick to that boundary from then on. I was tired of being flung back into the box of daughter over and over again, and little by little I began to overcome my old programming as I crept my way along into a life that was more truly my own.

In 2004, after seven years of struggling to make ends meet as a freelance editor and proofreader, I decided at 45 that it was time to find work that was a little more stable. I got a job as production manager with a firm that created testing materials for teacher certification. When I told my parents on the phone, my mother said stiffly, "Good for you." My father was silent. I would start in two weeks.

The next morning, my mother called again. "I've decided we're going to move out of the cottage now," she said, "And we need you to help."

For several months, she'd been talking about moving into an apartment in the main building of their assisted living facility in Illinois, saying that she couldn't care for my father any longer. Showing early signs of dementia, he would wander off occasionally, or ask her the same question twice in a row, and her patience was wearing thin.

I tried to explain that I would be starting my new job in two weeks, but she was adamant. "I can't do it any longer," she said. So I quickly made plans to go to Illinois the week before I started work.

I imagine that she felt I would abandon her as I got caught up in my new responsibilities, and I struggled against getting stuck in a replay of the time my parents dragged me back to St. Louis from California. My mother always got needier when I began to move forward in my life, as if she felt she was going to be left behind. I felt like a yoyo when it happened, spinning out into my life and being dragged back into theirs, wound up on the spool over and over. I lived in limbo as an adult, unable to get my life set up once and for all so it worked for me.

When I first went into their cottage on that trip, the air was soaked in a haze of frustration and depression, the heavy staleness of two people who had never been able to relate to each other on an intimate level and were now twisted into a macabre dance from which neither could extricate themselves. The house was clean, because my mother had hired someone the year before to come and clean once a week, and it wasn't messy; it just had huge amounts of whatever that stuff is that hangs in the atmosphere after an argument, the stuff you can feel as soon as you walk into a room.

I managed to get a fair start on sorting through items in the cottage in the first two days. Though my mother made halfhearted attempts to help sort through the accumulation of dishes and papers, and the odds and ends that my father had saved over the years, she wanted to spend a lot of time reminiscing and playing cards and generally commandeering my attention. Knowing that she needed to sort through her life as she made the transition, I listened and responded to her memories as best I could. I knew it was hard for her to give up her home, to know that this move would be the final one. I'm sure she remembered what Uncle John had said years before in his straightforward way when he moved into assisted living: "I came here to die."

By the end of the second day, I realized that most of the job would fall to me, and that the more my mother was there, the longer it was going to take. I already knew a week wouldn't be long enough; I would have to make at least one more visit to finish the job. And I knew that I would have to keep reinforcing my boundaries with my mother when I was there. If I didn't, I would have to keep going back forever.

When I returned home a few days later, I made plans to go back to Illinois the next month to try and finish. Luckily, my boss was very understanding.

My father was moved to the Alzheimer's wing for evaluation, and my mother moved into Jane Hutton Hall, a group of rooms for residents who could care for themselves. My parents would not be living together again, and that seemed to be a relief for my mother.

After my parents moved, the yanking on my psychic puppet strings intensified. I knew when my mother wanted me, even long distance. One minute, I'd be fine, focusing on whatever I was doing at the moment, and the next minute an image of her would flash into my mind with such force that it would tear my focus away from whatever I was doing and send my thoughts racing to Illinois. My stomach would drop like a skydiver without a parachute.

I was desperate to get the yanking to stop. One day I had the bright idea that my mother could find someone else to talk with—a minister or counselor—someone who could help her feel better, and ease the burden on me. The next time we talked on the phone, I suggested it to her.

"I don't need a counselor," my mother said. "I have you."

I knew my mother was going through a difficult time, and I wanted to help her just as desperately as I always had, but the interruptions were causing major problems for me. I couldn't focus for very long before my nerves started jumping, I had a hard time working, both at my job and at home, and I couldn't think about anything but her sadness and distress. No matter how hard I tried to force my thoughts in another direction, they were yanked right back to her. I began limiting our conversations, hoping that would help, but to no avail.

If there had been real love between us, I'm sure the whole experience would have been entirely different. I knew my mother had many friends at the Home, and nurses and aides to meet her every need, so I felt justified in limiting our conversations.

Where my mother was concerned, there was no room for what I needed. There never had been. When I came down with Lyme disease in 2003, I told my parents about it on the phone, and my mother brushed it aside. She knew nothing about it; therefore it was unimportant and she didn't want to know anything about it. But when a friend of a friend of hers contracted it a few years later, she realized how serious it was, and at that point she asked me, "Are you okay?" But by then, I had gotten back on my feet—with the help of neighbors and friends.

Everyone around me urged me to keep taking care of myself. And I was, to the best of my ability. But my health was still slowly declining. Between caring for my parents, making a living, and keeping a household together, I didn't have much time and energy left to care for me.

I discovered a few years later that neglecting myself was a huge mistake. It almost cost me my life.

# Chapter 12: The End of the Road

In early 2005, at the age of 89, my mother was diagnosed with ovarian cancer. She had lived with congestive heart failure after having a triple bypass when she was 82, but the cancer signaled the beginning of the end. Her doctor kept promising that he would try this medication or that for the cancer, and he and I even discussed surgery, but it wasn't an option, given her age.

When she was first diagnosed, I asked the doctor if he could give me a time frame, because I wanted to visit sometime before the end, but I didn't have the resources, financially or emotionally, to go to Illinois and spend the rest of her days with her. His best estimate was about six months.

In late March, I came down with a horrible case of the flu. My mother had been calling morning, noon, and night, and the strain was too much for me physically. Sinking into the depths of the flu, I slept most of the time, waking just long enough to have a pee and drink more water before going back to bed. The conflict between feeling sorry for my mother and trying to take care of myself was tearing me apart.

I even remember thinking incoherently in the midst of the worst of the flu that I had to die so that she could live. The tussle of competition had always been fundamental to our relationship, and throughout my life she had won every time. But some small part of me rebelled at the idea that I was supposed to die so that she could win the final battle, and that helped me gather the courage to pull out of the worst of the flu and start to heal.

Within a few days of my feeling better, she went rapidly downhill. Less than two weeks after I got over the worst of the flu, the nursing home administrator called from Illinois to tell me that I'd better come. I called the nurse's station in the wing where my mother lived, and they arranged for me to speak to her.

"Hi, Mom," I said carefully into the phone.

"Hullo." I could hear the resignation in her voice.

I didn't know what to say at a time like this. "How are you doing?"

"Okay."

"Jane called, and she suggested I come out to see you. Would that be okay?"

"Uh-huh." She already sounded far away.

"I'll be there in the morning. I hope you rest well."

I hadn't gotten any particulars from the nursing home director, and I didn't want my mother to hang on and wait for me if she was ready to go. I wanted her to feel as comfortable as possible about going through her death process in any way she needed to. "Mom? If you need to go before I get there, I'll understand. Okay, Mom?"

"Okay," she murmured. I felt like I was like talking to a four-year-old. I packed my bags and took the first flight to Illinois the next morning.

My birthday was the following week, and my mother had arranged with one of her friends to get me a fuzzy blue scarf. That afternoon, she pulled a bag out from behind the head of her bed, held it out, and said, "Birfday." Even in her suffering, she had remembered my birthday. I was touched and amazed.

The next two days were like a total replay of all the ways we had related throughout our lives. Shortly after I arrived, I pulled out a bag of peanuts—one of her all-time favorite foods. I had chosen the unsalted kind because of her high blood pressure and heart problems, and when she popped a couple into her mouth, her face scrunched up, and she said in a pained voice, "Don't ever bring me unsalted peanuts again."

Another time, she took my hand and pressed it to her cheek, and I knew she was telling me she loved me.

The first evening I was there, after my mother had gone to bed I felt the need to talk with someone who knew what was going on. I went to visit one of her friends, leaving the number where I'd be, and within less than an hour, the nurse called to say my mother wanted to see me.

I thought this was it. I walked over to the Home, my mind racing with images of holding my mother's hand and smoothing her forehead, telling her how much I loved her, and perhaps finally being able to relieve a bit of her suffering. I was even hoping on some level that maybe we could make some kind of heart-to-heart connection in her last hours, or achieve a measure of closure on the relationship, however minute or incomplete it might be. After a lifetime of discord, I was desperate for reconciliation with my mother.

When I walked into the room, the fire was back in her face, in her eyes. She suddenly looked very much alive. She said, "Close the door." I closed it, and turned back to her, ready to open my heart.

"You were over there visiting with Abby, and I needed you! I needed you here! You should be here instead of out having a good time with my friends!"

Her words hit me like a lead balloon, and guilt washed over me. I said, "I'm sorry, Mom, you were asleep when I left. And I wasn't having fun, she was giving me some support at a difficult time." I moved my hand to touch her shoulder, and she jerked it away from me, turning so that her back was to me.

"You should have been here, you should have been with me," she cried.

"I'm sorry, Mom. I'm here now." I waited, hoping that the finality of this time would let her allow herself to reconnect.

"I'm sorry, too." She pulled the covers tighter over her shoulders, her face turned to the wall.

I sat with her for awhile longer, until she drifted into sleep again.

It was the first chance I'd had since I arrived to just sit for a moment and let some of the tension of traveling and being with my parents again lift from my shoulders, drain out through my feet.

I look around the grayish beige room for the first time. It's a standard institutional room with one window, serviceable furniture, and a small, tired picture of flowers hanging above the bed. The oxygen machine's hum is loud in the small room. It gives a slight cough every now and then, like a small plane with one half-dead engine.

I sit and wonder how I can wrap up almost fifty years' worth of a difficult relationship, if not together with my mother, then at least for myself. There are no distractions in the room. I'm left alone with the stark reality of the disconnectedness we've always lived in, for all of my life, and more than half of hers.

My mother is so still. I've never seen her not moving. Her hands, her eyes, her face, her mouth were always moving. It's eerie, and as the oxygen machine drones along, I feel almost like I've been transported to some other dimension.

There are things I need to say, and I'm surprised by the opportunity the oxygen machine's loud hum offers me. I came expecting to give comfort and solace, and to take my own feelings back home to deal with later, as I always have. I hadn't expected the freedom to speak my heart. Somehow it seems to be the right thing to do. So much needs to be expressed. I ache with the need for peace and comfort, for some kind of resolution to it all.

I clear my throat and try to begin, whispering under the whine of the oxygen machine. I can't even hear myself, but it doesn't matter.

"I wish it had been different, Mom. I wish you hadn't needed me so much. All I wanted was a little love from you, just a little, some encouragement at least once in awhile, just to let me know I was doing okay."

That's more than I expected to say. But the words press on me. They want to be spoken, and there are more and more of them coming up, clamoring to find expression.

It's the first time in our relationship that I can speak my truth with no interruption whatsoever.

"You always had to be first, the center of attention. You never let me have my turn, you never gave me what I needed, and it's really messed up my life. You took so much away from me, Mom, and I wish I could have it back."

My chest is jerking, as if there are monsters in me that want to get out. I feel giddy and frightened all at the same time. More words pour out of me, indistinguishable against the white noise, but essential because I am saying what I need to say, in the presence of my mother.

Suddenly I wonder, can she hear me? There's no response whatsoever; she's lying on her side with her back to me, and her breathing seems even. I know that patients on the operating table are supposed to be able to hear what the doctors and nurses are saying, even though they're unconscious. Can she divine what I'm saying, in her slumber of anger?

I'm shocked by the realization that I don't care if she can. For the first time in my life, there's space for me, for my feelings, in a room with my mother. I feel as if I've been given a gift. The balance between the sense of freedom and the weight of the guilt I feel for finally speaking my piece when she's in this condition tilts back and forth. But I desperately need resolution.

To restore the balance, I offer prayers that her suffering might end, that the rest of her death process might be easy for her.

Now I am the strong one, the one who understands how things really work. I didn't see that before. Somehow, knowing this makes me more willing to offer the comfort she'll need when she wakes. It's late, and I'm sure she won't wake again tonight, so I head back to the motel, feeling a little lighter.

The next morning, my mother was sitting up when I came in, and the nurses were trying to get her to eat, but she had no appetite. My father was there, quietly sitting in a corner of the room and watching her. In the eight months since he had been moved into the Alzheimer's wing, he had recovered to an amazing extent, though he still had some slight signs of dementia. He was extremely well-groomed and well-behaved, and more logically conversant than he had been in years. At 89, he looked and acted like a recently retired university professor.

When he left for lunch, my mother said, "I don't like having him here. He's looking at me like he's waiting for me to die." She sounded like she thought he was politely gloating over winning the competition of who could live the longest. And maybe he was. It occurred to me what an odd thing it was that in the ten months since they had left the cottage, she had gone downhill so fast, and he had recovered so quickly. Did they have their own version of Spider Love?

My mother grew more restless as the day wore on, and I offered what comfort I could. The local minister came, and we held a beautiful end-of-life service, traveling in our minds and hearts with her to the gates of her new home in Heaven, where she exclaimed how beautiful it was. Compliments did not come easily to my mother, and I was surprised to witness some eagerness in the midst of her distress.

That afternoon, one of the nurses came to me and gently suggested that it might be time for my mother to go to the hospital. There were no hospice services yet at the Home, and the resources for pain management were limited. By this time, my mother was occasionally emitting cries of distress, and my father and I decided to move her to the hospital where her care could be more closely monitored and stronger medication could be given to ease her pain and discomfort.

She was furious that we had made the decision for her. She rebelled with as much gusto as she could muster. I stood in the hall, listening to her cries of anguish as the orderlies struggled against her wishes to move her to the gurney and out to the waiting ambulance. Understanding that movement might be painful, one of the orderlies asked me, as my mother's health care proxy, if he could administer a slight sedative. I gave my consent, and off they went in the ambulance.

I collected my things and followed shortly thereafter. My father elected not to come along. He said there was a presentation that afternoon at the Home on financial information that he wanted to attend. I didn't blame him for not wanting to come; watching my mother in her suffering was grueling. And I was relieved, too, that he didn't want to go—it would have taken much more energy than I had to transport him and his walker out to the car and into the hospital and deal with both of my parents in my mother's last hours. Maybe he even knew that.

As I got into my car, I barely noticed the gathering storm.

On the way to the hospital, I heard a siren wail as I pulled up at a stop sign. If I was going to get stopped for speeding, I thought, for once I had a valid excuse. I looked left, I looked right, I looked behind me, but there was no emergency vehicle in sight. With a start, I noticed that the sky to the left of me was a sickly shade of yellow, and I realized that the siren was a tornado warning. I stopped at the nearest occupied building to find out what was predicted for the ten minutes it would take me to get to the hospital. The occupants were moving to the basement; the tornado was approaching the town from the west. They invited me to join them, which I did. I wanted to get to the hospital in one piece, even if I had to wait awhile.

Sitting with strangers in the basement of an unfamiliar building was a welcome break from what I'd been going through in the last 24 hours. We chatted a bit, and they offered me a cup of coffee as they expressed their empathy for my mother and me in this situation. I deeply appreciated their presence for the few minutes we spent together as the storm raged outside. That experience gave me another gift as well: the opportunity to disengage for a few moments and notice that there were people in the world who cared. For a little while, I was safe from the storm that life always seemed to throw my way.

After the tornado passed, I was on my way. When I reached the hospital, my mother was relaxed and accepting, something I had rarely seen in my life. It was as if she had vented all of her fury on the way to the hospital, and was now comfortable in that lull that often follows great emotional upheavals, and violent weather. Or maybe it was the morphine.

Parents can be powerful beings to their children, even when those children are grown. As I sat with my mother in the hospital, I felt absolutely certain that she had created the tornado with her fury at being taken to the hospital against her will. Given our history, the coincidence seemed simply too potent to put aside. Now that she's gone, whenever I happen upon a physicist's comment that we can create reality, especially in times of high emotion, I'm reminded of my mother and the tornado that blew through when she was on her way to the hospital.

Perhaps one day we'll discover that an ability to affect the weather is part of the state of near-death awareness, that as the molecules of our bodies begin to dissolve and our souls reconnect with All That Is, we begin to disintegrate into and interact with the atmosphere around us.

While we waited for a room to be assigned, I sat and watched the machines jerk out my mother's irregular heartbeat and breathing. I expected them to stop at any moment. I remember thinking with detachment how interesting it was that I was watching a machine to try and discern how my mother was doing, because it was so unusual to have no clues coming from her directly.

I went with her as a nurse wheeled her on the gurney to a room, and she seemed relaxed and content. I sat with her until she fell asleep again. She didn't seem to want any physical contact, and I didn't offer any. It had been forced on her by so many people in the last several hours, and if I'm to be truly honest, deep down, some primordial part of me was afraid that touching her might somehow offer her the energy she needed to regain her health, and then everything would start all over again.

My mother and I spent the last part of our time together as we always had:  disconnected. It's possible that that's exactly what she needed in order to let go. I know it was for me.

I sat in her room until late in the evening, and she continued to sleep. When I finally left to get something to eat, I realized how terribly tired I was, so after I had eaten and visited my father to give him an update, I opted to head to my room and get some sleep. I figured I'd need some energy to deal with the morning trek to the hospital with my father. I had never witnessed anyone's death process before, and based on the fire I'd seen in my mother's eyes the previous night, I thought she would be alive for another day or two.

She died very early the next morning before my father and I got to the hospital.

I didn't fully comprehend the true irony of the tornado experience until the day of my mother's funeral. For years, she had said, "I'm ready to go anytime, and I'm going to have a lot of questions when I get there." The day of her funeral was a perfect spring day. The sun was shining, birds were singing, and the urn with her ashes in it, suspended over the grave, was creaking just slightly as it nodded ever so gently back and forth in the warm breeze. I thought about the tornado, and decided that she had finally gotten answers to her questions, and that she was happy with them.

Until the day my mother died, I did everything I could think of to fill the inner void I knew she had inside. Neither of us was ever satisfied with my attempts. It took me a long time to realize that it had never been my responsibility as her child to "fix things" for her, even though I'd always believed that it was.

After her death, part of my grieving process included remorse for not having been able to fix things and finally make her happy, and part of it included deep sadness for a childhood never really lived. Most of all, her death at 89 was a relief for both of us.

I felt my mother's energy once more as I was traveling home a few days later. I had to change planes in the Baltimore airport, which I had never been in, and in order to get from one plane to the other, I had to cross through a tunnel to get to another concourse. Instead of standard fluorescent lights, an artist had installed long light tubes in swirling patterns on the walls of the tunnel, brightly lit in a beautiful rainbow of colors that pulsed and cavorted rhythmically back and forth from one end to the other. The display was an amazing quarter-mile-long light show, a stark contrast to the world of grayish beige I had been focused on for the last week.

I stopped at the entrance for a moment, astonished, taking in the stunning magnificence of the moving art show, and I suddenly felt my mother's presence. Only this time, she was not depressed or angry or anxious. This time, I felt her looking at the new world around her with the same sense of awe and wonder I was experiencing. In my entire life, I had never seen my mother awestruck and enchanted by anything, and I imagine she was showing me that she was happy in her new life. I was incredibly relieved to think that finally, finally, she might have found some peace and joy. Reconciliation with my mother had come a little later and a little differently than I'd expected, but it did come.

As I compiled lists of people to notify and wrote thank-you notes to people who had sent flowers and made donations, I began the never-ending voyage of processing our relationship. For over a year, I couldn't answer the phone without thinking of my mother, and I expected her to pop back into my life at any time. But underneath it all, I was beginning to heal, to step out of the box of daughter and grow into the grounded, boundless self I had always wanted to be.

# Chapter 13: The Long Goodbye

My father lived for more than three years after my mother passed away. His decline was slow and painful as he moved into his 90s. The doctor had put him on medication for his dementia, but the only thing the medicine seemed to do was to make him fully aware of exactly what was happening to him.

I remember one phone conversation with him in which he cried, "Don't you understand? I'm demented!" He was painfully cognizant of losing his mind, bit by bit, thought by thought, along with physical control of his bodily functions, and there was nothing that could be done about it. As I had been with my mother, I was incredibly grateful that there were many good people at the Home taking excellent care of him.

My father took over the spider activity in the years after my mother passed away:  he called over and over, needing my attention. One of my journal entries notes that he left six messages in one day. I spoke regularly with the nurses who cared for him, asking for their estimation of how he was doing. Most of the time, their responses suggested that he was comfortable, doing well, and sometimes even enjoying the activities there.

More than once I thought to myself that along with being the only one who took care of my parents emotionally, I was also apparently the only one they shared their misery with. They kept up the public face of "Everything is fine" all the way up to the end. To my knowledge, they didn't even share their deepest feelings with each other, only with me. To me, that's what emotional incest is all about.

Several months after my mother had passed away, the company I worked for lost several large accounts, and I was laid off along with a number of other employees. At that point, I decided to start advertising my editing and proofreading services, wanting to build a freelance business. I hoped that my father and I could develop a closer relationship now that my mother was gone, and I tried to convey to him my excitement about striking out on my own. Taking over my mother's role of keeping me in my place, he told me loudly and in no uncertain terms, "You can't run a business!" The frustration of still feeling blocked at every turn clashed constantly with my deep sense of compassion for my father's plight.

I felt sorry for my therapist, but I had to keep turning around and dumping everything out in order to hold on to some semblance of sanity. She stuck with me through thick and thin, and helped me to experience the steady mirroring and secure attachment that I had missed as a child. During that time, I let go of a lot of anger—pounding couch pillows, throwing sticks and stones into lakes and rivers, and journaling, journaling, journaling.

Early in the summer of 2007, the director of the funeral home my father had chosen called one Sunday afternoon, and apologetically told me that my father had called to confirm that all of his funeral arrangements were in order, and to ask about euthanasia. He said that he'd explained to my father that euthanasia was not legal in the state of Illinois, and asked if I was aware of my father's emotional distress. I said yes, I had been for some time, and I had talked with his doctor about possible medications or other options. I asked the funeral director if he knew of any other resources that might be helpful. He was as supportive as he could possibly be, but like the doctor, he couldn't offer any options other than suggesting more medication.

I called my father to find out if there was anything I could do to help him feel better.

I tried to open the subject gently. "Did you call Mr. Bristol to ask about euthanasia?"

"Yes." His voice sounded very far away. "I wanted to find out about it."

I wondered if this might be his way of asking for permission to die, so I offered my consent in the only way I knew how. "You know, a lot of people believe that they can choose when they want to die," I told him. "In some religions, they believe that you can just decide it's time to go, and then you go. You can just make up your mind that you want to go."

"No, I can't!" He spoke more loudly than he had in months. "Only God can decide when we're supposed to go!"

With a flash of insight, I recognized the depth of his conflict. He had forcibly controlled things for his entire life, but the termination of his suffering was the one thing he could not control. It broke my heart to witness his complete helplessness battling his fierce desire to control the only choice he hoped he still had: the ending of his life.

"I'm getting off the phone now," he said. "It's too much of a strain to hear."

"Okay," I said. "I love you, Dad."

"I love you, too."

I knew there was no solution, but the next morning I called his doctor to see if anything could be done. If all of his medications were stopped, would progression toward the end of his life be quicker? Were there any other options? The doctor was no more helpful than the funeral director, but I was able to make clear to the doctor and to the nursing home my father's wishes that absolutely nothing more be done to prolong his life.

My father had told me once that when his mother had had a stroke, the nurses tried to force her to eat when she refused food. She closed her mouth and shook her head, and they tried to push the spoon in. When my father noticed it, he told the nurses not to force her to eat if she didn't want to. So, in the last years of my father's life, I made sure the nurses at the Home knew the story, and knew not to force him if he chose not to eat. Sometimes that's the last thing a person can control in their lives, and I believe that choice should be honored.

Years before, when my mother was still alive, the three of us sat at the kitchen table on one of my visits, having tea in square black cups with square pink saucers. My mother held the stage, as she always did.

"I asked the doctor what would happen if I just stopped all my medications," she said, her brittle voice bouncing off the polished wood of the table. She claimed that she hadn't felt right since her triple bypass at age 82. She kept saying she felt like two different people, and she couldn't get them to go together.

"What did he say?" I asked.

"He didn't," my mother replied. "He just said, 'Now, Jerry, you need to keep taking your pills, that's what's keeping you going.' And that's the problem. I don't really want to keep going. At least not the way I've been." She looked down at her hands in her lap, pitifully swollen with rheumatoid arthritis. "Sometimes I just want to give up."

My father stared at her, stiff-lipped and silent, always the stoic. My parents rarely talked about anything remotely emotional in front of each other, only when one of them was alone with me. That's how the yoke got so heavy.

My mother looked up with a shiny hardness in her eyes. "I can't fault Dr. Kevorkian," she said. He had been sent to prison the year before. "Sometimes it's just right to help someone end their suffering." I was glad she wasn't looking at me. That would have imparted a sense of responsibility.

My father stared at my mother, wearing his usual poker face. I wondered then what he thought about her admission of her desire to die.

I went to visit my father a few weeks after he requested euthanasia in the hope I might be able to perk him up or help him in some way. Dressed for the sweltering Midwestern summer weather in a nice, conservative, age-appropriate tank top and light trousers, I headed for my father's room, grateful to be out of the heat.

His first comment on seeing me was a disgruntled, "Well, you look casual!" But if I had dressed up, it would have been "You look fancy!" I couldn't win.

Things got even worse during the visit. His difficulty in hearing made communication nearly impossible, and he was critical of everything I said and did. All I could do was try to be present, try to let him know that I cared and that I was sorry for his suffering. How does one comfort a family member who is suffering beyond belief for months on end?

On the last evening of my visit, I took him out into the garden in his wheelchair.

> It's a lovely evening. The lacy fretwork of sunlight through leaves decorates the patio, and birdsong floats through the trees. My father points to a small metal sign stuck in the rich soil: "God lives in the garden."
>
> He says, "I like it here."
>
> I lean close so he can hear me, and reply, "Me, too. It's beautiful."
>
> We sit together in silence for awhile, and I notice him staring at the sign. Setting my own

belief system aside to offer comfort from his, I ask if he would like me to say a prayer. After a moment, he nods, and ignoring the unexpected flame of old anger in my chest, I move closer and put my arm around his shoulders. He bows his head, and I close my eyes.

I'm not sure exactly what to say, but I feel a powerful need streaming out of him, and I want to address it, to bring him some kind of comfort and peace. "Dear God," I hesitate over the word, but push on. "Thank you for the lovely evening, and for our chance to be together again."

My stomach is jumping. Will my prayer be good enough for my father, who has said thousands of prayers over his lifetime? "We ask that you grant us peace on our journey, wherever we may go. I ask you especially for peace for my father, who has lived a life in your service and helped others whenever and however he could." I have to clear my throat, and I feel my father's shoulders shake for a moment under my arm. "Bring comfort to his heart and soul, and be with him as he travels on from here. Bless us and guide us as we move forward into the unknown. Amen."

I can only manage a small breath, and I have to squeeze my eyes for a moment before I can open them. My father's head is still bowed. He looks so small and weak, and I see his white hands trembling on the arms of the wheelchair. I swallow the lump in my throat, and rub his shoulder for a moment. We sit silently again as the birds serenade us and the soft breeze flutters the leaves.

When it starts to get chilly, I wheel him slowly back to his room. On the way, I wonder why I always feel scared, confused, incapable, and angry around my father. And yet when I'm with him, somehow I always feel a need to be loving, helpful, caring, and giving. I don't know why, and I don't even know how much of either of those selves is really me.

My father was placed in hospice a few months later, and lived for almost a year after that. I'm fully convinced that his medications kept him alive past the point at which he had any quality of life left.

After my last visit, my father decided that talking on the phone was too stressful, given his difficulty in hearing. I sensed that he was pulling away, though I could still feel his angst and depression long distance, the same way I had picked up on my mother's.

Several times a week during that last year, I got home from work or errands to discover that the nurses at the Home had left a message on the answering machine. Since I was my father's health care proxy, they had to inform me of every change in medication and every incident, from falls my father took to drops in his blood pressure. Every time I saw the name of the nursing home on my caller ID, I would think, "Is this it?"

In early 2008, during the last eight months of my father's life, I started losing weight at an alarming rate. The fly had just about had it. I had always been thin—with 118 pounds on my 5'5" frame—but even though I was eating four or five good-sized meals a day, I still lost weight. I went to the doctor, but tests and scans found nothing. My body was sending me a very clear message in the only way it knew how: I was literally *disappearing*, and it was frightening. Alice Miller was absolutely correct when she wrote, "The body never lies."

My doctor set up an appointment with a gastroenterologist, and we discussed food allergies—of which I had numerous—and the possibility of parasites or disease. I had tests for thyroid deficiencies, for intestinal problems, CAT scans and ultrasounds. Nothing was found, and the pounds kept dropping off, no matter how much I ate. I began to feel as if I was fading away, as if my entire connection with the physical universe was wavering, becoming tenuous, as if I was drowning in some gray reality where nothing matters. Though I never fainted, I felt so weak that I would sometimes sit down just in case, and it was nearly impossible for me to focus clearly on anything. I wonder now if I was feeling my father's drift between this life and the next, his process of beginning to let go into nothingness.

I bought a scale, which I had never needed to use before because I was thin, and got on it every morning with trepidation. I watched the numbers go down even as I willed them to go up. I refused to buy new clothes that fit, because I knew deep in my bones that this emaciated body was not me, that there was something wrong, even if no one could diagnose it. I felt like some tissue-weight paper-doll image of myself, as if all the parts of me that I had identified as "myself" had evaporated into the mist of continued stress. I pinned pleats in my pants so they would stay up, and covered the full-length mirror in my bathroom. I tried not to notice the hollows and bones where muscle had previously existed. I was down to nearly 100 pounds.

That summer, I found a lump in my right breast. I didn't know whether it was growing, or whether I had only discovered it because I was so thin. After checking with my doctor, I went to a surgeon for a biopsy the following week. Even though there was no sign of cancer in the biopsy tissue, he advised surgery to remove it, in case that was causing my weight loss.

I remember the day of the surgery with excruciating clarity. I'd been instructed not to eat the evening before, and by the time I was settled in the pre-op room the next morning, I felt as weak as a newborn kitten. The nurse set up the pre-op medication, gave me the TV remote, and left. I finally let loose in my vulnerability, crying buckets for myself and my father, for the horrors on both sides of a body kept alive only with medication, but with no quality of life. I love the Jewish proverb, "What soap is for the body, tears are for the soul," because it reminds me that the value of expressing the pain that life sometimes brings has been understood for generations.

There was no cancer in the tissue the surgeon removed, for which I'm extremely grateful. So that still didn't answer the question of the lost weight. I added vitamins; I tried different foods. I slept more. I experimented with food combining. Finally, I contacted an acupuncturist, who suggested Chinese herbs. My body, which now makes its likes and dislikes known almost as soon as I put something in my mouth, *loved* the herbs. Whatever the mixture contained, it must have been the key to my recovery. Either that, or the spider had finally lost the strength to drain the fly. I started gaining weight almost immediately, and began to come back down to earth from the dreamlike haze in which I'd spent the last six months. It would be another half a year before I could take the pins out of my pants, but I was on my way.

On a Friday afternoon in that same month, one of the nurses called to say that my father was showing signs of giving up, and that he probably wouldn't last for more than 24 hours. In my condition, I knew the stress of making the trip and being with him in his last hours would be more than I could handle physically, so I chose to be with him in spirit rather than in person. That primordial part of me was still afraid that if I made physical contact, he would somehow get well and the merry-go-round would start all over again, but I knew in my heart that if he asked for me, I would go. Part of me still loved both of my parents, all the way up until they died.

I asked the nurse to relay to my father my love and my intention to pray for him, because I knew he wouldn't be able to hear me over the phone. I prayed for him off and on that evening and the next morning, and sent him thoughts of love and compassion. I struggled mightily with the conflict between yearning to finally be relieved of caring for my parents, and wanting to send as much love and light as possible to my father, to ease his transition in any way I could. He passed away quietly on Saturday afternoon.

When I got the call from the nursing home, tremendous relief swept over me at the thought of his release after years of suffering. I imagined him floating gently, completely at peace, having finally taken command over the last situation in his life he could control.

I hope with all my heart that by the time I reach his age—another forty years from now—euthanasia is a legal option for those whose suffering can only end in death.

My father died the day before my parents' wedding anniversary. When I mentioned the anniversary to the funeral director as we sat to plan the service, he said, "You'd be amazed how often something like that happens."

When I told the hospice nurse later that I felt guilty about not being there, she kindly said, "I think he might have wanted you to remember him the way he was when he was strong, not the way he was at the end." Then I was almost glad I hadn't gone, because I'm sure she was right.

Enormous relief swept over me for days after my father passed away. After seven years of caregiving, and the stress of being there for my parents emotionally for my entire life, I felt half-dead, as if the "Spider Love" had drained me nearly to death. Though I had to deal with the details of my father's estate, after his death I turned my primary attention to regaining my health and gaining back the weight I had lost, and within a few months, I succeeded. I was not altogether surprised that I could return to normal now that the spiders were gone.

My father's funeral service was held the week after his death, on his birthday, and after the graveside portion of the service was over, I stood at my parents' tombstone, praying in my own way for peace for both of them, and contemplating my relationship with them.

I was ashamed of the depth of relief I felt that my agony was over at last.

As I turned to walk back to my car, I thought how strange it was that this time, when I said goodbye, I could actually just leave, just make my very own decision to go, and nobody would stop me or jerk me back into their lives again. They weren't going to call me back for one more admonition, I didn't need to call them when I got home to tell them how the plane ride was, and my mother wouldn't be asking again in a few months when I would visit next.

I felt like I was finally having the last word after a fifty-year argument.

The box of daughter had begun to disintegrate, and I felt the possibility of peace opening up in front of me for the first time in my life. There was still some grieving to do—grieving for my parents, for their suffering in the last years of their lives, for the parents I wished I had had, and for all that I didn't have because of who my parents were—but now I finally had the chance to find out who I really was. For the first time in my life, my life was truly my own.

When I went through my father's things, my self-imposed guilt for "not being there enough" lifted when I found the stacks of cards and letters I had sent: birthday cards, Easter cards, Halloween cards, anniversary cards, Thanksgiving cards, Christmas cards, get well cards. My presence had been with him even though I hadn't been there in person, and if it were at all possible for him to know I cared, the cards and letters showed him that.

Eleven months after my father passed away, I dreamed that he had been living with me in my apartment. I never saw him; I only knew he was living in my space because I saw his shoes, and the newspaper was open to his favorite page: the financials. His presence permeated everything.

In the dream, one day I came home, and he was gone. All of his things had been removed, and his presence had evaporated. I woke with the realization that I had carried him in my psyche for a long time, and that I'd finally achieved enough peace about the horrors of the last years of his life that I could let him go.

The dreaming human psyche is amazing. It squirts out bits and pieces of our pasts to cook our lives with.

Though there weren't any weather-related events right after my father died, two days before the first-year anniversary of his death, Hurricane "Bill" moved up the East Coast, where I was living at the time. Though my father's father called him William, he was known as Bill throughout his adult life. It would have suited my father's dry wit to send a reminder of himself on the anniversary of his death.

I've always believed in synchronicity; and given the intensity with which my parents lived their lives, going out as a tornado and a hurricane makes a weird kind of sense to me. Either that, or I have a bizarre psyche that creates weather based on what I'm feeling at the time.

Many months after my father died, I was stunned to learn that scientists had discovered a possible link between narcolepsy and psychic ability. I wouldn't have been surprised to find out that my father was psychic—in the last several years of his life, I felt him yanking on me psychically in the exact same way my mother did. Now I wonder if his obsession with finances and numbers served to keep him focused on the physical world, so that he didn't get distracted the way I did by all those unspoken thoughts flying around.

At the funeral services of both of my parents, many people made a point of coming over to me and telling me what wonderful people my parents were. I listened to one person after another rave about all the things my parents had done for others, and how pleasant and polite they were. I nodded, and agreed, and said, "Oh, isn't that nice." By that time, I had done enough work that I could hold on to my own truth even as I listened to others wax poetic about all that my parents had given. I could keep my truth, and not spoil their inspiring memories by telling them about my own.

In fact, my parents truly were amazing people in many ways, and I wish I could have known them outside of the destructive connection we had. My mother was vivacious and spirited, and my father always put others' needs in front of his own. They were both tremendously creative, and throughout their last years, they continued to volunteer and to help others in any way that they could. I'm sure that if I had met them outside of our family, I would have been intrigued by their lives, and inspired by their focus on giving.

Life is a paradox, and my parents were right in the middle of it.

\* \* \*

# Chapter 14: Out of the Box

I remember thinking, as I drove away from the cemetery after my father's funeral, that now I would have the chance to be anyone I wanted to be. I could be totally free to do what I wanted and change my life in any way I chose. It was exhilarating, as if the entire Universe was suddenly open and available for me to grow into.

All my life, I had felt as if I'd been living only half a life—always watching other people living, and waiting for my turn. Finally, it was my turn. But I completely underestimated the power of the unconscious mind to repeat patterns from the past in an effort to "fix" them. It took more than two years, and two moves—one to a different state—before I began to feel confident that I was leaving my past behind.

The first thing I discovered was that I was a little afraid of unearthing my passion and applying my strength and power to goals and objectives. I'd never had a chance to explore my personal power in life, except in my acting. With the fear of being steamrolled fresh in my mind, I encouraged myself to take small steps forward rather than hopping in giant leaps.

Even as I tentatively moved forward, I kept bumping into old issues. They were still there, hanging out in my psyche, waiting to trip me up at the same time they were trying to protect me from harm. When I had an experience that acted as a "trigger"—meaning that it brought up repressed memories and feelings, and caused me to fall back into old patterns—I paid particular attention to whatever situation had activated my backslide. As time went by and I gained clarity on more and more of my issues, I noticed that some of my friends behaved in ways that reminded me of one or both of my parents, and as a result, old fears and feelings were triggered as I related to them. But I was determined to overcome the old patterns, and I doggedly kept working to see everything with more clarity.

I was excited to notice that when someone tried to manipulate me, I became aware of it pretty quickly. Usually, I got a little angry once I saw through the game, and that connected me to unconscious anger at my parents for training me to be a doormat. Once I released the old anger, I could go back to the friendship with more understanding.

One day I realized with a flash that dealing with my mother's manipulation was at the core of my general confusion in life. Things had gone haywire throughout my life on a regular basis, and on that day I realized that the reason confusion was so familiar to me was not because I didn't cope well with life, but because my mother was very good at creating chaos. I don't know whether or not it was a conscious act on her part, but it nonetheless had a huge effect on my ability to move forward in my life.

With this new realization, it suddenly became very clear to me that a large part of my difficulty with life came about because whenever I started to move in a new direction, or when I finally achieved something, my mother had done whatever she could to wrest my attention from what I was doing and place it back squarely on her. And when other people manipulated me, the confusion came over me like a wet blanket because the situation was so familiar. The old pattern sat right in front of my face, laughing at me.

I saw that my mother had always stepped up her manipulation when I began to move forward in my life, and because my sense of self was weak, I got confused by it every time. After years of getting muddled by my mother's manipulation, my brain had translated the experience into a generalized belief that things always got messed up when I tried to move forward in my life, instead of noticing that my mother continually threw a wrench into the works to keep me in second place.

I worked to develop a habit of consciously reminding myself that it wasn't that I messed things up, or that the Universe created a lot of obstacles to what I wanted, it was rather that my psyche was used to having everything spiral into chaos. The chaos was what I had always noticed—because it was so familiar, and so dramatic—more than I noticed when things went well in my life. I absolutely believe what I often read: that what we focus on expands.

My mother was locked in an eternal struggle with life. She struggled to get what she wanted, to change things when she didn't like them, to push things in the direction she wanted them to go. If things didn't go her way, it became a catastrophe in her eyes. Even though my father let her have her way most of the time, she still struggled—because it was her habit.

And I learned the art of struggling both from her role-modeling and from my relationship with her. Struggling "against" held the attraction of "life as drama"—it made life feel more intense and exciting, made it feel like I was living fully and with relish, when what I was really doing was falling prey to the same "drama addiction" my mother did.

The way I see it now is that since any excitement about life or exploring things or considering possibilities was forbidden, all the excitement there might have been about growing and exploring got turned into bad drama and catastrophizing.

One morning after my parents were gone, I woke up and realized that I didn't have to struggle any more, that I could actually *flow* with life, let it unfold, and just accept things as they came along. I could do my best to make life what I wanted it to be, but the rest of the time, I needed to let go. I was so used to struggling that when I let go, life almost felt boring. But letting go of the struggle also allowed space to open up for more growth, and for new and exciting activities and relationships.

After worrying for my entire life that catastrophes were everywhere waiting to happen, and that the other shoe was always threatening to drop, I finally reached up in my mind and took it down. Now, when I notice that shoe up over my head, I remind myself that I don't need to struggle, and that small problems are not catastrophes. Life is so much more peaceful without the drama addiction.

It was incredibly intriguing to observe my inner self over time, as the layers of denial fell away to reveal the hidden aspects of myself that I'd repressed. It was like becoming un-schizophrenic, pulling all of the fragmented parts of my personality into a whole for the first time in my life. It wasn't until I began to integrate all the parts of myself that I realized how fragmented I had always felt, how many roles I had always played, how many parts of myself had been repressed. And as I rediscovered all the parts I had lost touch with, a gift came along with each one: my passion for life was reawakened, I learned how to enjoy things again, and the desire to connect with others on an intimate level resurfaced.

Sometimes, I learned something new.

In early 2010, I had been trying for weeks to arrange a short vacation, but things kept getting in the way. The pattern of things getting in the way was still so familiar to me that I didn't notice I was once again locked in a struggle with *nothing*, resisting my mind's insistence that everything had to be done before I took a vacation, that I shouldn't spend the money, that I had to get an oil change first, ad infinitum. I finally decided it was now or never, and made plans to go. Six hours after I made the reservation, my throat was burning with the early warning signs of a cold. Not wanting to give in and give up my treat all over again, I determined to go anyway.

Ten minutes into the trip, I burst into tears. As I looked inside to figure out what was going on, I discovered that part of me was horribly frightened at the prospect of making the trip, even though it was less than a three-hour drive. I had taken many trips on my own before, so there was no logical reason for my fear.

As is my habit, I started a conversation with that part of myself to figure out what was going on. I know it sounds crazy, but it's the only way I know of to get in touch with the repressed parts of myself, the aspects of my psyche that went underground when I created the Good Little Girl façade.

> "What's the matter?" I ask myself.
> "I'm so scared to go."
> "Who am I talking to?" This is my way of finding out what part of my psyche I'm dealing with, as my adult self takes on the role of empathic witness.
> "Kathy."
> "How old are you?"
> "Two. I'm almost three." This is the youngest "voice within" I've ever heard. Her description of her age makes complete sense; my birthday is a few weeks off.
> "What are you afraid of?"
> "It's too big. I can't go. I'm too little."

At this point, I usually explain that I'm an adult now, and I totally understand what that part of me is going through. I tell her that I can handle lots of things now, even if she feels she can't. I imagine myself taking her hand or giving her a hug, comforting her and making her feel safe.

The tears come faster. I have to pull over to the side of the road.

"You're such a good girl," I tell myself, still holding on to the empathic witness viewpoint. "You always try so very hard, and nobody even notices, do they?" I'm crying harder as this part of my psyche releases some of the pain it's held for almost fifty years. "You do things so well, but nobody ever tells you that." I wish I'd brought more Kleenex. "I'm so sorry."

Then a memory flashes into my mind, one that I had been aware of before, but had never seen through this little girl's eyes:

I'm two, almost three, and my parents have brought me to an Easter egg hunt for two- to-four-year olds in Forest Park. I hear the signal to start, and I'm running, running, really fast, and I see an egg here, an egg there, and I grab them. I'm running from one bush or rock to another, finding all these eggs, picking them up and putting them in my basket with a sure touch, until the basket is almost full. In the memory, I can see almost everything clearly, and out of the corner of my eye I notice a little boy, chunkier than I am, with blond hair, who must have just learned how to walk, because he's toddling slowly and awkwardly down the sloping hill. Excitement rises inside of me as I notice my basket getting full, as I feel the power I have to move so fast, find eggs, and grab them.

Suddenly, my mother catches my arm. "Honey, that was a siren," she says. "It wasn't the signal to start. We have to put the eggs back."

But I'm sure it was the signal. I show her my full basket, hoping she will share my delight.

She picks me up, carries me back to the starting line, and gives my basket to the man who's leading the hunt. My stomach hurts, and I want to cry. Finally, I got something I wanted, and it's being taken away.

After the hunt, I remember my father carrying me to the car. I'm holding my Easter basket, and it has three eggs in it. I'm sad as only a two-year-old can be, and my sense of my own power and speed curls up to hide in a corner somewhere, not to be seen again for many decades.

Either my parents didn't notice my distress, or, if they did, they just wanted it to go away. In any case, on that day, little Kathy learned a number of lessons: 1. Even if I work really, really hard, I still can't get what I want. 2. Even if I do get what I want, someone might take it away. 3. Being powerful and fast and smart doesn't really pay off.

In essence, it doesn't pay to succeed.

As I sat in my car by the side of the road watching this memory through new eyes, I digested the weight of learning these lessons at such an early age. "You deserved to have all of those eggs!" I said to myself, and I decided that when I got back from the trip, I would get little Kathy a huge basket of eggs for Easter.

The trip proceeded without incident, and I had a nice vacation.

Several days later, when I brought the plastic eggs home, took them out of the package and filled a basket to overflowing, I was surprised to discover a feeling of glowing amazement as my inner child realized I was giving her something she had always wanted. From that moment on, I began to feel more free to succeed, to move forward, to allow myself to reap the benefits of my work. Helping the child within me feel acknowledged, understood, and comforted has been a major part of the huge task of rebuilding my life.

I know the inner child can be healed. All we have to do is treat him or her like we would treat any other child.

In the months after my parents died, I discovered that in order to truly be myself, I would have to go against their wishes—to essentially disobey them—and to fully face the old fear that danger lurked whenever I did things in my own way instead of theirs. I had to get comfortable with disobeying the unseen and implicit rule that I could not live my life in my own way, and I had to disobey the rules I'd been taught about how life should be or how I should behave. Then I had to go forward with the knowledge that yes, I'm going to feel like I'm disobeying, but it's right to move forward anyway, because most of what I learned from my family was flawed and twisted, and I have an absolute right to live my life in my own way.

My inner child's belief that I would be destroyed if I disobeyed still exerted tremendous power over the part of my psyche that's linked to the survival instinct. Though I felt silly, I kept reassuring myself that I wasn't going to die if I did things my own way, and eventually I began to feel more comfortable with my own needs and desires.

I've often wondered how many writers and artists who came into their own late in their lives had to wait for their parents to die before they felt safe enough to explore and express the gifts within them.

In that first year after my father died, I just wanted to hide—as I had wanted to hide from my parents for twenty years. I wanted to move to some remote place where no one would ever need me again, and swath myself in layers and layers of blankets to muffle the outside world, so that I could finally grow enough psychic skin to protect myself from needy people.

As a child, there had never been space for me, because my mother took up most of it with her intense and hurried energy, and my father took up the rest with his loneliness. Now, all of a sudden, there was an infinite amount of space for me to grow into, and at fifty-one, I didn't know how to start.

I had straddled two worlds for so long—my own life path and my parents' world—that I didn't know how to plant both feet solidly in my own life. The one thing I knew was that I wanted the process of discovering myself to be as organic as possible, because I had lived pretty non-organically for my entire life. To begin, I had to figure out how to let go of living in the shadow of my parents' expectations, and stop making the kinds of choices I had made for most of my life to protect myself from their criticism.

I had internalized their hypercritical voices into a rock-solid judge in my psyche that heaped condemnation on almost everything I did: "You should have done it that way!" "Of course it didn't work, you should've known." "You can't do that, you're not good enough."

I tried everything I could think of over time to quiet those voices or get rid of them somehow, but they were well and truly rooted. I finally discovered that the only way I could stop those voices from ruling my life was to shout them down in my head, over and over, until they finally shut up. Wryly, I realized that I was doing in my head what most people would have done with the actual people in the actual situation. So it was second best, but it worked.

I spent many months processing the feelings, the thoughts, the events, the relationships that I hadn't had time to process when I was small. I walked in the woods a lot. I discovered that Alice Miller's suggestion of creating art was very helpful, and for some reason, working on jigsaw puzzles seemed to be the thing that most helped me to process all the old stuff and integrate the new. Many times, I found that an urge to work on a puzzle meant that my psyche was working to integrate an experience or aspect of self, and insights would come rapidly as I came close to completing the puzzle. Most important was to allow time and space and solitude for letting the process of healing evolve, and to be a compassionate witness for myself as it unfolded.

As I unraveled the past, I began to discover who I wasn't. That was the first step on the road to finding out who I was.

# Chapter 15: Unraveling

Until I was well into my forties, I had held myself and my life together by being the Good Little Girl, the false self (as psychologists call it) that my parents brought me up to be. I had had moments, and even days or weeks at a time, where I felt I was living more from an authentic core, operating out of my own values and beliefs, living in my own rhythm instead of my mother's. But the false self had always helped me hold my life together, and as I worked to put it behind me and live more authentically, my entire life began to unravel.

I had learned as a child to ignore my competence and intelligence unless I used it in a way that pleased my parents. All of my life, I had been split in two: my competence, my confidence, my ability to handle life was part of the Good Little Girl persona, and my vulnerability, sensitivity, passion, and creativity were facets of who I felt myself to be deep inside. I had to figure out how to become competent and confident without relying on the Good Little Girl façade. I needed to integrate all these aspects of myself in an organic way so that I could become whole.

Until my parents passed away, I'd always felt only half alive, wrenched back and forth between masquerading as a robot and working to overcome my conditioning so I could create a life based on my own values and desires. I had never felt whole and entire unto myself. Now that I had the time and energy to focus on discovering myself, I felt as if I were scraping layers of rust and dirt off of long-unused farm equipment, and trying to figure out how to oil everything and get all the parts to work together again.

I worked with two wonderful therapists over the years, one in New York, and one in Massachusetts, who painstakingly helped me unravel the tapestry and see through the illusions that were instilled in my childhood psyche. Both spent countless hours listening, and both were extremely supportive, helping me with reality checks and encouraging me to find a way of life that worked for me. They helped me break the prison of secrecy surrounding my family's dysfunction, helped me get out of the cage I'd grown up in.

I was very lucky to find them, and I'm extremely grateful to both of them. Without them, I would never have experienced others who believed in me and supported me, who were on my side over the long haul. In many ways, they helped to make up for the lifelong lack of support from my parents.

In therapy, I uncovered myself over the years, piece by piece, layer by layer, until I began to have a vague idea of who I might be. I had trouble trusting the authentic self that was emerging from within me, because I had always identified with the Good Little Girl, even after I knew she was a façade. Because she was my safety net, I fell back into her role when things got rough. I didn't know how to create a life based on my own desires, because most of my life was still a reflection of who my parents wanted me to be.

I spent a lot of time sorting through the facets of my identity as I'd known them up to that point, trying to discern which values and beliefs were truly mine, and which ones I had unthinkingly adopted from my parents. I wanted to discern how much of my worldview was based on my own experience, and how much was mindless mimicry.

Because my parents created the façade of a fine, upstanding family in public while the dysfunction raged behind closed doors, I had a difficult time exposing the dysfunction and deception, even to myself. I was so well trained to keep my family's secrets hidden that I even hid them from myself. But I kept at it, discovering one secret after another, until they began to fit together into a massive, crazy psychological jigsaw puzzle.

I paid particular attention to beliefs that were nearly invisible, like the belief that I always had to be "good." That belief was extremely difficult to unravel, because the real me is a conscientious person who believes in and practices kindness and nonjudgment as much as I can. But where is the line between that and being a Good Little Girl, a doormat who allows everyone to walk all over her? Whenever I had an urge to do something good, I'd ask myself, "Is it real, or is it Memorex?"

I asked myself how much of my identity was a reflection of who my parents were—which aspects of myself I had developed merely to provide the psychological mirror for them that they needed in order to feel okay about themselves. One of these aspects was a habit of gloominess. I had struggled with depression for most of my adult life, and in thinking about my relationship with my mother, I began to recognize that one of the things I'd had to mirror for her was her depression. That meant *I* had to be depressed. How much was hers, and how much was mine?

I remember one morning in particular, a chilly, gray day in April, winter's last gasp. I slumped over the sink as I washed the breakfast dishes, trying to get up the gumption to start on the day. Suddenly the sun broke through the clouds, stretching shining beams down to the earth like angel slides. It didn't affect me one bit. Still in a slump, I went for a walk, and my mood lifted; but when I got home the mental fog came right back. I asked myself why, and realized that I was so used to feeling depressed that when my mood lightened, it was an unfamiliar and slightly scary feeling.

As I dug underneath that concept, I discovered a fear that if I got into a good mood, someone would pop up and drag me back down into the gulley of despair. Unthinkingly, I had fallen back into depression simply because it was a habit—a habit I'd developed decades earlier so my mother would have someone to keep her company in her misery. From then on, whenever the gloominess descended for no reason, I reminded myself that I didn't need to mirror my mother any more, and that she wasn't coming back to drag me down, and I would quickly find my way back to a much better mood.

I know my mother loved me in her own way, but except for very few occasions, all I ever felt from her was her frustration and disappointment with life.

Pondering the possibilities helped me to comprehend whether certain aspects of my personality were truly a reflection of who I am, and I eventually discovered that many of them were not. Understanding how deep the mirroring process had been was extremely enlightening, and I began to feel as if shards of assumed identities were falling away, bits and pieces of who I thought I had been that I had only believed were "myself" because my parents needed me to be a certain way. The sifting and sorting process was massive, and the more I proceeded, the more I came to see that there had not been very much of "myself" throughout my life. Most of my living had taken place through my parents' framework and expectations, in the box of daughter they had built for me.

But my mother was right in one sense: I am sensitive. Dr. Elaine Aron describes me to a T in her book, *The Highly Sensitive Person*. I may be more sensitive than is good for me, but I would rather be aware of my feelings than wander through life without being much affected by what goes on around me. I would rather revel in a beautiful sunset and be able to relate to someone else's pain than be immune to feeling. I would rather do battle with the ghosts of the past than live a life of quiet desperation or develop a disease because my body can't take the repression any longer. I was born with the urge to grab life with both hands and gobble it up, just like my mother. She gave me the gifts of intensity of feeling and passion for life, and I would not be the same person without those gifts.

I discovered that what was most important in my healing process was just to give myself space—to explore, to feel, to make choices—and to let my instincts lead the way even when they seemed to direct me toward unusual and unfamiliar vistas. I learned that variety is truly the spice of life for me. I enjoy new experiences, and a large part of what keeps me going in life is seeing new sights, whether it's window shopping in a new store, or visiting a new town.

Each new thing I find that works for me adds a measure of happiness to my life and a further elevation in my self-esteem.

Every time I followed an urge that wasn't part of my false self's view of the world, it inevitably led me to a deeper piece of my real self. I learned that it was all a matter of trusting myself. Since I never learned how to live life on my own terms, I had never learned to trust my own perceptions.

Recognizing that I actually could and absolutely should trust myself was a great and protracted lesson. I finally found the courage to start trusting my own impulses, and allowing myself to follow them even when they were contrary to what I had been taught. Developing that trust in my instincts turned out to be the key to healing for me.

Since I didn't have much of a frame of reference for how to operate authentically in the world—how to live life, how to make decisions, or how to keep my life functioning smoothly—all I could do was keep exploring and moving forward into the darkness of uncertainty, whether I knew where I was going or not. Eventually, I began to feel connected again to the self I had been as a very young child, before everything got confused and covered over and frightened into hiding.

The strength and tenacity of my psyche's imprinting of early experiences often amazes me. When I have an experience that's reminiscent of the past, and the old programming begins to resurface, it feels like I'm trying to bend steel with my mind if I attempt to oppose it. Often, it's my psyche's way of bringing up an outmoded approach to life that's getting in my way, or an ancient behavior or thought pattern that needs to be examined. As I observe the information that my psyche provides, and release old feelings surrounding the past, the old programming emerges less and less often.

The deep memories of abuse may never go away, but as I work to integrate my feelings, the memories are relegated more and more to the past, and my life becomes more and more my own creation.

It soon became clear to me that going back to the bee's nest during my parents' last years and observing my reactions was an integral part of my healing. After I'd been in therapy for some time, every time I visited my parents I noticed huge jumbles of feelings cascading through my body, more than I could sort at the time; but once I got home again and processed them, they provided me with a very lucid understanding of what I'd gone through in childhood.

Each time I returned home after a visit, foggy-brained and full of crazy emotions, I released the pent-up feelings by shaking my hands and head, thwacking pillows against the couch, and finding ways to let go of my anger. Tearing up newspaper was the best way I found to express my vexation. Allowing myself to express my feelings provided tremendous relief from the constant tension of having to care for my parents, and I'm not sure I'd have made it through without that outlet.

Over time, I began to understand that a large part of my confusion about who I was came about because my mother had projected disowned parts of herself onto me—qualities that she didn't want to acknowledge within herself—and then responded to me as if I were those parts. When I tried something new and my mother said, "Do you think you could do that?" she was removing her internal doubts about her own abilities and pasting them on me. Then I became the failure, and she could be perfect. Her insistence that I was too sensitive may have been an attempt to deny some of her own feelings—and may actually have created even more sensitivity in my system as I unconsciously tried to live up to the self-image she gave me.

I never knew from one hour to the next which role I was supposed to be playing: her savior, her slave, or her scapegoat. When I look back, I realize I didn't feel "real" as a child, but I had no idea I was playing different roles. I believed in the illusion just as much as she did, because I had no other way of viewing the world, no sense of identity outside of my relationship to her. It was as if my mother lived in my brain, still in control even when I wasn't with her.

I often wonder if the alternate meaning of writer's block is "Somebody in your psyche is getting in the way of your being able to express yourself."

As I sorted through memories, trying to distinguish between facets of myself that felt authentic and those which were imposed by my mother, I saw that my mother had also seized aspects of my life, enfolding them into her behavior as if they were her own. This behavior fed my confusion about where I began and where she ended. For instance, when I suggested a new craft project, she wasn't interested, but days or weeks later she would say, "I came up with a new idea," and it would be mine.

When I lived in New York, I found a wonderful perfume called Jil Sander No. 4. I was enthralled with it, and when I went to visit for Christmas, as soon as I got off the plane, my mother said, "You smell nice. Is that a new perfume?" She had loved Jean Naté for years, but her preference changed in that instant, and she began referring to Jil Sander as her perfume.

Every year after that, when I asked her what she wanted for her birthday, she'd say, "I'm running out of my perfume. That's what I'd like for my birthday." There was no sense of sharing something we enjoyed; she just took it over as if she had been the one to discover it in the first place. The perfume became her signature scent, and I became the one who was using her perfume.

Perhaps she adopted things like the perfume in an effort to be more like me. But it always felt like she was taking a piece of me away, and after so many years, there was very little left of me. The process of sifting and sorting allowed me to reclaim those aspects of myself that my mother's behavior had erased and consumed.

On my birthday in 2011, an off-season tornado raged through the St. Louis airport, shattering windows and causing significant damage to Concourse C, the terminal where I had met my parents for more than 15 years when I flew in to visit them. The tornado caused very few injuries, and no one died.

I wondered why: why it happened on my birthday, why that particular concourse sustained most of the damage. I'm constantly amazed by a Universe in which such synchronistic events take place.

I sought out photos and video footage of the damage with as much rabid interest as I had investigated BPD. I saw pieces of ceiling that had fallen on chairs that I had actually sat in. The passageways where I had reluctantly walked with my parents at the beginning of a visit were strewn with debris. A sick thrill ran through me as I viewed the damage, and I felt the fury of the tornado rise up from within me, an emotional nausea I had repressed for two decades so that I could allow myself to be a psychological slave for my parents. I discovered deep wells of rage at how my parents had used me and caused me to grow up feeling defective, unlovable, incapable, and inept.

Within two days, I developed a fever and swollen glands; my body threatened to get sick as a dog if I didn't acknowledge and let go of the anger I'd been holding in for over fifty years. I shook my fists and pounded pillows, and contemplated historic figures like Lizzie Borden and Jack the Ripper, imagining their release of fury as they hacked and slashed, and I felt a little less alone in my rage.

When I had finally expressed the anger I needed to let go of, the rage subsided, and I sought the soothing energy of the ocean.

> As I walk up and down the cliffs, listening to the roar of the surf and the calls of gulls, I try to figure out how to go on from here carrying this grief that my parents couldn't give me a strong foundation in life, and how to accept the fact that I will never get what I need from them, because they're gone.

It feels so terribly unfair that I gave them all I had—almost to the point of killing myself—and that I received so little attention in return. I look at the gulls, bobbing on the water, and wonder whether animals weigh what they have against what others seem to have, or whether they ever feel incompetent. I don't imagine they do. I imagine they just accept whatever is happening, and accept whatever they're feeling as perfectly suitable for the circumstances. I would like to be like them.

I want to just release my rage in one big blazing ball of emotional fire so I never have to look at it again. But fifty years' worth of criticism and abuse is a bitter pill to swallow, a hard thing to forgive.

The sound of the waves rushing the shore soothes me, and I think about how differently I would feel if I could give up this burden of anger, so it wouldn't pop up again every time "somebody done me wrong," whether it was someone I knew, an organization, the government, whatever. I can get a little taste of the freedom offered by surrendering that old load, but the child within me wants something in return, some kind of payback. The best I can do at this moment is to let go of whatever I can, and trust that the process will continue until I'm free.

I imagine my rage floating out of me like a blood-tinged mist, drifting away over the sea, displaced by the wind into tiny molecules, and eventually dissolving. The sun and surf bring a whiff of peace, however temporary, to my soul.

On the drive home, a tenor is singing a lovely aria in German. I don't understand the words, but the music is so sweet and his voice so tender that I feel like the Universe is singing a golden lullaby to me, stroking my bruised and battered heart with devoted comfort. I think about how art and music heal the holes in the human soul that we create with our own dysfunction.

Because of my parents' abuse, it has taken me many years to learn that I can trust myself, and I still sometimes have trouble trusting my own judgment. My mother's constant questioning of my decisions, even after I reached adulthood, imbued the roots of my decision-making process with uncertainty, so that even now, when I'm certain I'm certain, there's still a wee bit of doubt that I'm really and truly certain. The only way I've found to circumvent the problem is just to tell myself, "This is what I'm going to do, whether it ends up being right or wrong." If I add my intuition to my logic in making a decision, I can usually find the best choice for me.

For most of my life, I thought people would hate me when I did what I needed to do for myself. The insidious effects of emotional abuse derailed my life's journey and tore holes in my sense of self, and I know that those wounds will be healing for the rest of my life.

At the same time, I realize it must have been terribly difficult for people of my parents' generation to have come of age during the Great Depression, and to have lived through so many incredible changes during their lifetimes. Both of my parents suffered due to their own life circumstances, and I know they did the best they could. I can't place the blame squarely on them. They treated me the way their parents treated them. The true perpetrator of the emotional abuse I experienced is a generations-old method of upbringing by indoctrination, the instilling of fear, and the discouragement of every natural instinct a child has.

In my head and in my heart, the twin flames of rage for how my parents treated me and compassion for their suffering still fight for coexistence. It's such a paradox to hold those two feelings at the same time, but it lets me know that I am human, and gives me hope that I've attained a respectable level of awareness.

I hope that one day, I will finally be able to turn to the light and fully embrace compassion—perhaps even forgive my parents completely for what I know in my heart was misguided, unintentional behavior. For now, whenever I think of them, I say a little prayer that they have finally found peace.

The Buddhist way, which I've always admired, suggests observing the entire picture with compassion. In order to view it in its entirety, I must look at both my parents and myself with compassion, including in that picture my deep and intense feelings about my parents' behavior. And as Alice Miller suggests, I must understand and digest my rage and indignation in order to become a fully functioning adult.

Through the process of facing and integrating my anger, I have destroyed its hold over my emotions and my interactions with others. And I've begun to weave a new and satisfying tapestry for my life.

# Epilogue: Journey to Wholeness

After I had unraveled most of the old tapestry, I was left with threads of so many colors that I didn't have any idea how to sift and sort them into any kind of order, or whether I even needed any of them at all to weave a new tapestry for my life.

As I combed through the threads and gained more clarity on the worldview I had learned from my parents, I began discarding values I'd inherited from my parents that I didn't truly believe in, like the idea that life is supposed to be miserable. I thought a lot about what I did believe in, and what I wanted to believe, and I wrestled fiercely with my psyche as I worked to let go of the past and change negative beliefs.

I realized that I had to figure out how to unhook my identity from the Good Little Girl and the other roles I'd always played, so that there was room for me to create a new identity based on what I wanted my life to be.

Some of the values my parents had held dear I still believe in: be kind to others; do good works that benefit the community; conserve energy whenever you can; and reduce, reuse, recycle. So there were some threads I wanted to keep. But eventually I learned that even if I espoused some of my parents' values, I could still create my life however I wanted it to be.

After fifty years of living in the box, sometimes the notion that nobody can get in the way of what I want anymore still surprises me.

I was determined to ignore the old voices, and to value my good qualities—to appreciate myself when I lived from my own truth. I resolved to focus on what I did well, and on the positive qualities that I had, rather than fretting over mistakes and misunderstandings. I learned to forgive myself for not being perfect.

As I focused on building my confidence and encouraging myself to believe I could succeed, I noticed that people began treating me with more respect:  asking my opinion, listening to what I had to say, even inviting me to speak in front of groups on occasion. I could almost feel the old neural pathways in my brain sizzle into nothingness as new ones took their place. With persistence, my life, my worldview, and my world began to change to conform to my new beliefs. I finally learned that when you change your worldview, you change your whole world.

My cat has been a significant thread in recreating the tapestry of my life, one nourishing, nurturing relationship that I can count on for as long as she lives. An abused kitten that I rescued when she was almost a year old, she taught me that trust is built one small step at a time, and that love is the most important and nurturing connection in life. If I'm honest with myself, I realize that in spite of never knowing what love felt like as a child, I have learned what it feels like from my relationships with animals. And I've always found nourishment by being out in nature. Plants and animals are completely nonjudgmental, just totally themselves. To me, they represent a physical manifestation of the nourishing energy of the Universe that permeates all things.

My relationship with my cat eventually became an unveiling of my deepest, purest, most tender self, the one I've always been giving attention to when I've loved the cats I've known. Somehow, I invested this most beautiful, vulnerable part of me into cats so I could offer that part of myself the love I never received. As I began to understand that I had projected my child self onto cats, I learned to have compassion for the little one who still lives within me, who wanted so desperately to make her parents happy that she put all thoughts of her own happiness aside and became a fly for them.

I helped her understand that it was okay to do well, to have fun, and even to win, by playing computer games. Nobody got jealous, nobody got upset, and I only had to compete against myself. It seems odd, even to me, that I had to consciously learn how to win because I had never felt safe winning anything before, but it's just one more example of how my childhood experience was responsible for gaps in my development.

I wonder how many people with low self-esteem think of themselves as "losers" simply because it was never safe for them to win.

As I did some research on childhood trauma, I discovered that my brain and nervous system developed differently from people who had less stressful childhoods: my system was trained to function according to the whims of other people. My brain did not develop circuitry that would help me explore new possibilities, problem-solve effectively, or be aware of what I needed and focus on building my own life. I've been able to "rewire" my brain and nervous system to some extent as an adult, but it takes patience and vigilance to exercise the rewiring and ignore the old blueprint.

In *The Biology of Love*, Dr. Arthur Janov points out that some of the structures in the brain don't develop properly when a mother has little emotional rapport with her baby. He suggests that the prefrontal cortex—the planning, thinking, logical, integrating portion of the brain—is impaired by a lack of early love, and may not function to full capacity later in life

Reading his words made me realize how difficult the struggle toward competence and success can be for people whose low self-esteem arises from a difficult childhood. Dr. Janov's words helped me to accept myself more fully. It's not that people with low self-esteem are lazy or unintelligent; the problem may be that their brains are wired differently than the brains of people who were appreciated, deeply connected with others, and successfully success-oriented from early childhood.

But my early experiences have also provided benefits. One of the great strengths I developed in response to my early years is a vivid and extensive awareness and understanding of emotions, both my own and other people's. I can make connections between circumstances and emotional responses that most other people wouldn't be aware of. The challenge of viewing life from within this emotional structure is that I have to be careful not to get derailed by the emotions, but rather do my best to let them help me guide myself on my life path. I know that if I didn't have the sensitivity that I do, I wouldn't have the resulting gift for insight and understanding.

Another aspect of sensitivity that I appreciate is a healthy attunement to the natural world and human instinct. I can feel the thirst of the trees in a long summer drought, I sense when storms are on the way, and often I've experienced extreme feelings of being unsettled, only to discover a day or two later that an earthquake occurred somewhere on the other side of the planet. This is another aspect of living life as a "thin-boundary person."

I usually know when someone is trying to deny or cover up their feelings, and with my deeper understanding of our very human emotions, needs, and instincts, I can see through the cultural illusions which coerce us into unnatural actions and conforming behaviors, and turn us against what truly lives in our hearts.

Up until 2011, I still struggled with the fear that my parents would somehow return, ruin everything I had accomplished, and drag me back into their world. I was pleased to discover one day that the fear they would return had disappeared, and I knew that the very last part of me had finally realized they were dead. Apparently, the knowledge had to sink into my psyche through layers and layers of self, of memory, of fear, until every last particle of me was certain they wouldn't return.

So much of life happens under the surface, where we don't see it unless we're paying attention: bad moods that happen for no reason, fatigue that won't go away even with rest, relationships that fail time after time. The answers are hidden in the fragmented mosaic of the psyche, just waiting for an invitation to come out and help to solve the problem.

One day, after receiving yet another "Thanks but no thanks" response to a piece of writing I'd submitted, I felt a lump in my throat, and stopped what I was doing to take a moment and explore what was going on inside. From deep within emerged an anguished certainty that no one had ever wanted me for who I was. I realized that the rejection of my writing represented the rejection I had experienced throughout my life in my relationship with my parents.

As I grieved the ache of feeling that I had never been wanted, new understanding took the place of the pain. I saw that when the feeling of being unwanted was hidden in my unconscious mind, it created a major stumbling block in my quest for success. With the belief that I wasn't wanted for who I was underlying my efforts to market myself as an actor, then as a writer, it was hard for me to believe that other people would want to cast me or read my words. I realized that my discomfort had probably affected my working relationships in those fields—that my repressed feelings had caused me to unconsciously sabotage myself.

And I also finally realized that what I had thought was a deep love for my parents was primarily a fervent *longing* for their love. Though there were things that I loved about both of my parents, when I looked at the relationship with clarity and the distance of time, I realized that the attachment I felt toward them was largely a lifelong hope that one day I'd be able to get them to love me for who I was.

Like any other codependent relationship, my connection with my parents had been a ghastly blend of love and pain in which needs and desires escalated out of control, and the façade of "helping" and "loving" was often a disguise for controlling someone's behavior. I was drawn to my parents like a moth to a flame, unable to fly away even though I continually got burned. Once I faced the truth of what our relationship had been, I was able to accept myself without condition, because I saw through the deception and I understood how different we had always been.

The hidden treasure inside of me began to unfurl when I focused on my truth, and on the qualities I valued in myself. I was becoming whole.

My body has become very clear in letting me know what it needs, and I've become better at deciphering its language. When I feel a cold coming on, if I stop and pay attention, I often discover that all I really need is a good cry. I'm still amazed at the idea that a release of tears, of old sorrows and long-held grief, can not only allow much more space in my life and open my brain to new possibilities, but can also help my immune system overcome an onslaught of germs. According to Dr. Aletha Solter's book, *Tears and Tantrums*, there are a number of studies that have found a relationship between crying and physical health (p. 18). Apparently, crying removes stress hormones and toxins from the body, restoring a state of equilibrium. It also improves emotional health.

Alice Miller wrote in her wonderful books that painting was her way of accessing her childhood history; that it helped her to express her child's rage and indignation over what had happened to her, and helped her to heal the wounded child within. For me, the primary method of release has always been physical: dancing, clenching my muscles, stomping, shaking my head and my hands and my body when emotions threatened to overtake me, throwing myself into yard work or cleaning, punching pillows (I always brushed them off and fluffed them up afterwards), and tearing up newspaper when the rage at how my parents treated me bubbled up and demanded expression. Sometimes I could feel the old energy dissolving as it left, like finally expelling a held-in breath. The release of emotions allowed me to let go of the physical memory of trauma trapped in my muscles.

I expressed my feelings like this in private for over twenty years, and the process allowed me to go back into the world as a "normal" human being, each time a little more aware of what happened, each time a little more free from the past and more able to move forward in my life. It also prevented me from displacing my emotions onto other people, the way my parents dumped theirs on me. And sometimes, it brought huge revelations.

I woke up angry today. The back and shoulder pain I've been struggling with for weeks is worse than it's ever been. A shard of memory surfaces: my mother's voice on the answering machine pleading with me to call her again because she's feeling down; the pull on my body as I struggle to balance my needs with hers.

Anger at feeling used for so many years overwhelms me. My body wants to thrash, to obliterate the old sense of being impeded from living my own life. I open the window and shake my head, my hands, letting my legs and body tremble and wiggle as the feelings discharge. My body feels like a Gumby body, rubbery and loose, bones following muscles as the energy of anger surges away from me. I grab a pillow from the couch and shake it, gritting my teeth and growling as I let go of the rage that spurts up from within.

With a flash, a new thought emerges from the depths of my unconscious mind: for the last two decades of my parents' lives, I absolutely hated being in contact with them. How could I not have known that? My tongue sticks out as I let go of the emotional nausea attached to this revelation. The back of my neck clenches as I become aware of the weight of the unconscious burden I've been carrying, and as I continue to shake my body, the pain in my back begins to subside.

As the day wore on, the revelation turned into horror: how could I have put up with doing something I hated for twenty years? I was aghast. I knew I hadn't particularly *wanted* contact, but I had apparently repressed how much I hated it. Being the Good Little Girl was the only way I could respond to them, and when I was the Good Little Girl, I had to bottle up my feelings, because that was part of the role. Apparently, I had to repress my sense of being the fly so that I could continue to provide support for my parents.

I spent a day or two assimilating that sensation of horror, bouncing it around in my brain and seesawing between feeling aghast and relaxing into the relief that I didn't have to do that anymore. A few days later, I had processed the insight, and my back and shoulder pain were gone.

Not too long after, I read John E. Sarno's book, *Healing Back Pain: The Mind-Body Prescription*, in which he postulates that back pain is almost always an expression of repressed anger, and that once the emotions are acknowledged, the pain, which has acted as a distraction, disappears. I'm always amazed at how efficient my system is at processing and clearing old, tangled feelings, as long as I let the process happen as organically as possible.

There were times that I resisted expressing emotions, or held myself back from trying to understand the pain, but then I got off track and ended up lurching back into the fog of depression and uncertainty, mired in the emptiness of the abyss until I began paying attention to my inner world again.

I finally admitted to myself that even though I'd wanted to stop having contact with my parents for those twenty years, on a primal level I had just been too afraid to make the break. I believe wholeheartedly in Alice Miller's hypothesis that we carry the infant's fear of our parents' wrath under the surface of consciousness until we bring it to light and release it. That's the only way I can explain my continued fear of annihilation in the face of the fact that my parents were no longer strong enough to cross the many miles and punish me.

Unconscious programming is extremely powerful. I expended tremendous energy to keep almost fifty years' worth of repressed feelings under wraps, and the strain almost tore me apart. I couldn't acknowledge the depth of my anger and resentment while my parents were alive, because they were good people, and I felt like a monster for being so angry at people who had done so much for others.

In those last twenty years, I developed an allergy to one food after another: first to wheat, then to milk, to corn and soy and yeast and oats and nuts. The truth was that I felt "allergic" to my parents during the last years of their lives, but there was no way to express that to myself. But, again, the body never lies. My allergies, and the unexplained weight loss I experienced in the last year of my father's life, were my body's way of trying to express my truth. It took more than a year after my father's passing before I could begin to understand what it was trying to tell me.

As I listened to my body, I began to understand how battered I had felt when my parents manipulated and criticized me as they tried to control my thoughts, feelings, actions, and even my self-image. Though I understood the reasons behind it all, my knowledge didn't diminish my anguish as I finally allowed all of my painful feelings to surface, and began again to grieve the past and let go of it. I tried to have compassion for myself as I came face to face with my true feelings, which came pouring out every chance they got once I opened the gates of my psyche.

Walking through the pet store with cans of cat food in my arms, I notice a little white mouse scampering around his exercise wheel, and I stop to watch, hoping to pick up a bit of energy and enjoyment through my connection with animals. He's very cute, with a little pink nose and ears, and tiny blue eyes.

But after watching for a moment I notice that he keeps looking up. He's not just exercising, he's looking for something. The wheel keeps going; he keeps running; but every now and then he tries to crawl up the back of the wheel, and finally I realize *he's trying to get out of his cage.* He wants to run free—he wants grass and bugs and tree bark, he wants the freedom to go where he wants without being confined to a stupid wheel that only goes round and round. My chest gets hot and my throat fills with recognition of another creature who is trapped in a box and can't get out. I barely make it out of the store before the tears come, another release of the throbbing ache that still comes up when I remember what it felt like to live in the box of daughter for fifty years.

From time to time, I've contemplated the idea of giving up my work of releasing the past, because it seems an endless, massive task. But with each episode of letting go, I am more aware, happier, more unlimited, more comfortable in my own skin and in the world. The gifts I receive for having done the work are immeasurable.

I imagine people wonder, why didn't you just stop? Once you saw what was going on, why didn't you just say no to the abuse, or leave, or fight back? But one of the characteristics of someone who has been abused is an incredible sense of smallness—physical, mental, emotional weakness—and often, a feeling that there's no one to help, no one to offer support, no one to be on their side. Abused children feel like they can't even trust a hand that reaches out to help, and that feeling continues right into adulthood. The abuse has chopped so many pieces from their confidence over time that it feels as if there's nothing left of the self but a shell, so fragile that it could blow away in a high wind.

Many people deny some of the darker feelings they have toward parents and others who have abused them, and sometimes they act out those feelings on partners or children, as I believe my parents did. From my perspective, that's one of the reasons our society seems so crazy. Too many people are trying to deny too many powerful, unexpressed emotions. Alice Miller states that if we're honest with ourselves about our emotions, we find that our feelings always have some basis in truth, and I wholeheartedly believe that. The hard part is being honest.

I'm not proud that I have had so many negative feelings about my parents. Somehow, the fact that they were so good to so many people makes the way they treated their children all the more abhorrent, yet seems to absolve them, all at the same time. They weren't just bad people who abused their kids; they did a lot of good, helped a lot of people, and lived within their own code of honor and integrity. That makes me feel guilty about my anger. But I also know that my anger is justified: both of my parents used me, and probably used my brother, to meet emotional needs that weren't met in their spousal relationship, a situation termed "emotional incest" by therapists. That's another name for "Spider Love." The emotional incest I suffered at my parents' hands caused the loss of my childhood, and though I believe I can heal completely from the trauma, I will never be able to recover that time.

I may have spent more than forty years of my life living in a false self, but I'm grateful that my spirit was never broken. Sometimes I'm distressed that it took twenty years to unravel the twisted tapestry of my childhood, but those years of work uncovered great chunks of the self I was truly meant to be.

Developing relationships with other people takes time and energy and focus, but for people who have been abused, developing a relationship with the self also takes time and energy and focus, because that relationship never grew naturally, the way it does with children in more functional families. It took time for me to learn to trust myself in ways that people who are not abused can trust themselves from early on in life.

People who have been emotionally abused may not have memories of physical brutality and bodily pain that survivors of physical abuse suffer, but the damage is just as intense, and takes just as long to integrate and heal. The scars are internal, buried in the psyche, in the mental and emotional structure that forms the basis for the self's interaction with the world. When a child has been emotionally abused, healing can only come about when the self learns to trust its own perception of how things happened.

For me, the rhythm of healing has become a balance between taking time to let go, and moving forward: focusing when I need to on the darkness, the pain, the frustration, until it's fully expressed, and then letting it go and turning toward light and laughter and friendships, the wonderful possibilities that life has to offer. In listening to myself, I have found my own balance between dark and light, and learned that they must coexist if I'm to be healthy and whole.

Life consists of both light and dark, and over time I've come to realize that although there may be perfect moments in life, there is no way to make everything perfect. Once I accepted that there would always be some darkness in my life, the dark shadow of my unconscious no longer controlled me.

I know that I could have gone ahead and lived my life without examining the past, without working through the painful issues. I could have avoided the entire odyssey, and spared myself the grief, by just ignoring and denying everything. But then there would have been no joy, no love, no real sense of connection with others and with the world. I never would have discovered who I really am; I never would have learned to love myself. I would have continued to live in the box my parents created for me, depressed about the wasteland that my life seemed to be, disliking myself and feeling weak inside and wondering what was wrong with me that I couldn't enjoy life or achieve success the way other people seemed to.

I've known many people who've made the choice to ignore the past, and it's just as valid a life choice as unraveling the tapestry. But it wouldn't have worked for me. My body just can't lie and be healthy at the same time.

I'm not afraid of the frustration of not being able to control life; I'm not afraid of tears, of mistakes. I'm afraid of going back to the state of monotony and numbness that cost me so many years of my life.

My lifelong goal is to create a beautiful mosaic of a life from the broken bits of a traumatic childhood, a light-filled stained-glass window fashioned of the shattered shards of the self I've excavated.

I wonder: does everyone try to fit the pieces of their lives together as if they're working on an unfamiliar jigsaw puzzle? Or only those of us who were so disassembled that most of the pieces don't even match?

My psyche continues to offer hope in the form of dreams. In 2010, I dreamed that my parents, who had been living with me in the dream, had decided of their own volition that it was time to move out and find their own place. The dream was simple and matter-of-fact, but it showed me that I was letting go of the old relationship within the deepest part of myself.

I'm convinced that the only way to leave our pain behind forever is to face it, feel it, and finally let go of it. Dr. Christiane Northrup's words, "emotional incision and drainage," are a perfect description of the process. My willingness to face the pain and work to release it has been the primary source of my healing. I have fought my demons face to face, and I may have lost some battles, but I'm winning the war. It's been an incredibly long journey, but it is extraordinarily worth it to finally feel good about myself.

The fear, the pain, and the memories of abuse are mostly behind me now. My brother and I are taking steps to forge a new relationship. Every day, I'm stronger, happier, healthier, and more able to accomplish what I set out to do. My life works well for me, and I'm full of gratitude that I found a way to let go of the past so its shadow no longer threatens me.

I'm finally taking my turn, and looking forward with anticipation and hope to whatever life may bring from this point on. After a lifetime of wondering who I really am, I've found the self I was meant to be. I'm finally free of the box of daughter, and I like who I am.

# Acknowledgments

I offer my deep appreciation to those who read the manuscript in the process of writing it: Ning Sullivan, Tom Foster, and Alana Cox, and to everyone who offered their support as I struggled to put my experience into words: Jewel Davis, Emily Rosemary Thompson, Peg Hafertepe, Mimi Watroba, and workshop participants and leaders at Writers in Progress. Thanks also to Susan A. Schwartz and Jennifer Caven for their encouraging and insightful editing and critique.

I am most grateful to the many friends who supported me through the last difficult years with my parents: Joyce Coté, David James, Betsy Newton, Joy Kaubin, Beverly Rhodes, Nadine Benzaia, and numerous others. I would not have made it through without their patient understanding and support.

Many thanks to the staff at Maine Authors Publishing, who answered my questions with infinite patience, and to the many authors before me who have determinedly championed each person's right to live their own life with confidence, strength, and happiness.

# Bibliography and Recommended Reading

Aron, Elaine, Ph.D. *The Highly Sensitive Person*. Broadway Books, 1997.

_____. *The Undervalued Self*. Little, Brown and Company, 2010.

Beck, Martha. *Steering by Starlight: Find Your Right Life, No Matter What!* Rodale Books, 2008.

Bradshaw, John. *Healing the Shame that Binds You*. Health Communications, 1998.

_____. *Homecoming: Reclaiming and Championing Your Inner Child*. Bantam Books, 1992.

Engel, Beverly. *The Emotionally Abusive Relationship: How to Stop Being Abused and How to Stop Abusing*. Wiley, 2003.

Evans, Patricia. *Victory Over Verbal Abuse: A Healing Guide to Renewing Your Spirit and Reclaiming Your Life*. Adams Media, 2011.

_____. *Controlling People: How to Recognize, Understand, and Deal with People Who Try to Control You*. Adams Media, 2003.

Forward, Susan. *Emotional Blackmail: When the People in Your Life Use Fear, Obligation, and Guilt to Manipulate You*. Harper Paperbacks, 1998.

_____. *Toxic Parents: Overcoming Their Hurtful Legacy and Reclaiming Your Life*. Bantam, 2002.

Golomb, Elan. *Trapped in the Mirror: Adult Children of Narcissists in Their Struggle for Self*. William Morrow & Company, Inc., 1995.

Greven, Philip. *The Protestant Temperament: Patterns of Child-Rearing, Religious Experience, and the Self in Early America*. Alfred A. Knopf, 1977, p. 37 (see in particular, Part Two: The Evangelicals).

_____. *Spare the Child: The Religious Roots of Punishment and the Psychological Impact of Physical Abuse*. Alfred A. Knopf, 1990 (see, in particular, Part IV: Consequences).

Janov, Arthur. *The Biology of Love*. Promethius Books, 2000, p. 18.

Jawer, Michael A. and Marc S. Micozzi, Ph.D. *The Spiritual Anatomy of Emotion: How Feelings Link the Brain, the Body, and the Sixth Sense*. Park Street Press, 2009.

Johnson, Robert. *Owning Your Own Shadow: Understanding the Dark Side of the Psyche*. HarperSanFrancisco, 1993.

Lawson, Christine Ann. *Understanding the Borderline Mother*. Jason Aronson, 2002.

Matthews, Arlene Modica. *If I Think About Money So Much, Why Can't I Figure It Out?* Summit Books, 1991.

McBride, Karyl. *Will I Ever Be Good Enough?: Healing the Daughters of Narcissistic Mothers*. Free Press, reprinted 2009.

Miller, Alice. *For Your Own Good: Hidden Cruelty in Child-Rearing and the Roots of Violence*. Farrar, Straus and Giroux; 3rd edition, 1990.

_____. *The Body Never Lies: The Lingering Effects of Cruel Parenting*. W. W. Norton, 2006.

_____. *The Drama of the Gifted Child: The Search for the True Self*. Basic Books, 2008.

Shengold, Leonard. *Soul Murder: The Effects of Childhood Abuse and Deprivation*. Ballantine Books, 1991.

Solter, Aletha, Ph.D. *Tears and Tantrums: What to Do When Babies and Children Cry*. Shining Star Press, 1997.

Wood, Amy. *Life Your Way: Refresh Your Approach to Success and Breathe Easier in a Fast-Paced World*. Modern Sage Press, 2010.

# Reader's Guide for The Box of Daughter

1. For the person who chose this book: What made you want to read it? What made you suggest it to the group for discussion? Did it live up to your expectations? Why or why not?

2. What do you think motivated the author to share his or her life story?

3. Do you think the author is trying to elicit a certain response from the reader? Was the book what you expected it would be?

4. Discuss the book's structure and the author's use of language and writing style. How does the author draw the reader in and keep the reader engaged? How did you respond to the author's "voice"?

5. Were there any instances in which you felt the author was not being truthful? How did you react to these sections?

6. Did you feel that the author's story mirrored your own life experience in any way? How?

7. Compare this book to other memoirs your group has read. Is it similar to any of them? Did you like it more or less than other books you've read? What do you think will be your lasting impression of the book?

8. In what ways do you think the author's story is reflected in our culture and society? Do you know others who have had similar experiences?

9. What did you like or dislike about the book that hasn't been discussed already?